MW01489824

# Secrets of the Soul Biography of an Abused Child

By Sam Shelley

XULON PRESS

# Part 1

# Secrets of the Soul Biography of an Abused Child

# Part 2

# Healing of the Soul
## Where Compassion and Love Triumph

## By Sam Shelley

# Dedication

I dedicate this book to my beloved and cherished husband Michael Kenny, to my granddaughters Harley Jo and Hannah, along with the many friends who shared their similar stories with me. I pray that they find freedom from their past of abuse as they set out on their own journeys to bring about innocence to their future generations.

# Table of Contents

# Foreword

As a shepherd of God's people, I have had the opportunity to work with several people who have undergone the effects of abuse on families, and how unhealthy it is to not deal with the God given feelings in the healing process. As one of the editors of this book, I was given a first row seat into what the author has experienced and how the power of the living Lord Jesus has made an impact at changing her life from a life of fear to certainty. Sam has had a great opportunity to not only author this book, but she has taken what she has learned and used it to help others through her mentoring and training of others. I trust this book will help unlock the truth of God's Word in new ways as you seek to be free in Christ. Thanks for the chance to be a part of your life. May God bless you and your family as you continue to grow in Him.

Sincerely,
Frank Moyer, Pastor
Celebration Community Church,


"'There is no pit so deep, that God is not deeper still'" Corrie TinBoom. Sam's open, honest, heart touching book about her life is a testament to these two verses; "I am the way, the truth, and the life no man comes to the father but by me" and "Know the Truth and the Truth will set you free". True to her

God given nature, she wants to help others by sharing her personal story. As a sister in the Lord and as a teacher I recommend this book highly. Lord, bless those who read this book and continue to bless its dear author, Sam.

Marie Hayes


Dear Sam,

I have read your text which you dropped-off for me and I am excited about its contents. It helps me to understand the things you went through, which fortunately, you were able to uncover all by yourself.

Now that I have read the manuscript, I understand the insight you have gained, and I think this would be a great help to others in making themselves well. This is almost a "self-help" manual, and I think that you should definitely get this published, because I can see it would have great use for people who have been abused.

The text which I have read seems like a classical presentation on behavior modification that occurs with childhood molestation and abuse. You are lucky that the Holy Spirit has given you insight, and you certainly have talent to express your feelings.

I also want to thank you for sending me the initial manuscript because it helps me in understanding patients who have similar problems, and I think it will be useful to other patients as well. This text should be shared with others who have similar problems.

Sincerely,
Donald J. Jacobs, M.D.

# Preface

This was not an easy task, however, I felt the persistent urging within me to write my story. I contribute that nudging to the Lord Jesus Christ who gave me the courage to face the abuse perpetrated upon me at a very early age. Jesus came into my life when I was twenty-five years of age and from that moment He directed my path to honesty and truthfulness. As I faced the truth relevant to my birth family, I found God's boundless grace, enabling me to forgive my abusers and to let go of the traumatic pain and anger that I held deep down inside.

Pondering over the journey of my youth, it is as if my story is about another person's life. As for me, I've been healed from the attacks on my character and body. So why wade through all these memories again? Because of this statement, "Blessed be God, even the Father of our Lord Jesus Christ, the Father of Mercies, and the God of all comfort, Who comforteth us in all our tribulations, that we may be able to comfort them who are in any trouble, by the comfort with which we ourselves are comforted of God." (2nd Corinthians 1:3&4, NKJ)

That scripture from Corinthians tells me that I went through such pain and trials of life so that I would be equipped to help others to find the strength needed to undergo the inner healing from the pain and hurt within them. I can truly say that if not for what I went through, I would not be the person I am today. I am not stating that what I went through was right, but what I went through gave me strength and courage to fight for who I am, who I want to be, and who I am meant to be.

I have an urgent need to get my book in the hands of other victims so they too can find an inner peace and be able to escape from their hellish inner self that keeps them on an emotional roller coaster. This keeps them away from the person God created them to be before someone changed the outcome of their innocent lives by betraying them through abuse.

The hardest part of sharing my story with others is that I feel almost victimized again because I am laying my whole self out in the open, being naked before an audience, and that may bring about perilous times to me because of the nature of this book. However, if one person can find his/her way out of the pit his/her mind has them in, then lying naked before you will be worth it all.

Part two of this book was written ten years after part one. In part two there are noticeable changes in me. I faced a lot of emotional upheavals and plenty of soul searching between parts one and two. Over time I was able to forgive the people who abused me and also to forgive God for allowing the abuse to happen. Love triumphed over my fears, anxiety, and hatred toward the perpetrators. Forgiveness takes time. Each person is different; however, a victim needs to come to the point of forgiveness so that as a survivor he/she can move forward in life.

I have changed names and places to protect the future generations in hope that they may find a way to escape from the malady of abuse and hopefully be able to keep their innocence. Names were changed in order to protect those that thought they were doing right, for example, the abortionist doctor who believed my mother's lies in order for her to cover up molestation. Places and names have been changed to protect many non-family members who were also victims of this society and its shortcomings.

I suggest that you have pen or pencil in hand and when emotions are triggered you stop and write in the margin what you're thinking or experiencing. This will aid you in opening the tunnel of your mind in areas which you may be hiding. May God be your guide and the healer of your past and may you come to the end of your journey being whole and complete. The truth will set you free. "And ye shall know the truth, and the truth shall make you free." (John 8:32, NKJ)

# Acknowledgements

God has put some extraordinary people along the pathway of my journey as He guided me to accomplish this book. The first is my spouse and very best friend Michael Kenny who believed in me and encouraged me over the last thirty-eight years to be all that I could be and who loved me in spite of my many shortcomings. My daughter and second best friend, Brandy who received her degree in criminal law and psychology who in turn helped me to understand the dynamics of many of my behaviors. I give honor to Dr. Donald Jacobs, M.D. who laughed and cried with me as I struggled through many of life's happenings and was always there for my family and me. I'm grateful to Professor Lapoint who encouraged me to find my voice to write and did some editing for me. I credit Pastor Frank Moyer who initiated my working with other victims of abuse and also edited my writings. I thank Elouise Rossler who was the final editor.

# PART 1

# Secrets of the Soul

# Chapter One

# CUPID

It was soon to be my forty-fifth birthday and my parents wanted to know what they could give me as a special gift. I asked for the picture of Cupid that still hung over the bed I had slept in as a child. There was something intriguing, yet tumultuous about that picture. I hung the picture next to my jagged white rock fireplace. Murkiness and trepidation hung over the picture like a black cloud. With intense consciousness I wondered what it could be that fixated such a distressing sensation within me as I felt a nauseous queasy feeling in my stomach. Little did I know that the secrets Cupid and I shared would be revealed and relived in the abyss of my mind.

Cupid is my best friend. I don't know exactly how to explain her or tell you where she lives, and she's kind of mixed up about the day of her birth. I have lots of dolls. They are my babies. Someday I will get married and have real babies and Cupid will live with us. Cupid is not like my dolls; she's real. She's different than my friend Cindy. Cindy has to knock when she comes to my house, but not Cupid. Cupid just appears when I need her or when we want to have some fun together.

Cupid and I have gone on some great adventures together. The big fields where we played had some old car wheels that rotated like steering wheels and fastened to telephone poles. In the winter the wheels and poles were used to hook a heavy rope onto them for the purpose of pulling the children and their sleds or skis up to the top of the sledding and ski hill. The county would then take the telephone poles down for the summer to prevent neighborhood children from getting injured. Together Cupid and I dragged them and made a make-believe vessel that we played pirates on. Cupid let me be the captain. She talked like she lived way back in that time era because she knew so much about being on a ship. Sometimes I thought we were really sailing to all the places Cupid described. At times my playmate Cindy from across the street played with me on the ships, but Cindy thought playing pirates was boring. I wish Cindy could have heard Cupid tell the stories about being lost at sea and found by Captain Novak. How could anyone find sailing boring?

Cupid loved to shoot arrows and she never missed her target. I loved to watch her. What I could never understand is that she never ran out of arrows and she hardly ever went back to pick them up, but somehow her quiver was always full.

I practiced for weeks, shooting arrows into a bale of hay, trying to get as good as Cupid and my brother Ben. However, shooting at a bale of hay was as boring to me as Cindy's trip to the sea. One day, when there wasn't anyone around, I borrowed Ben's hunting arrows and went to the field. I had his quiver around me, and I shot every arrow straight up into the sky. I couldn't believe the strength I had as those arrows pierced the heavens and arched back down like a rainbow, and then fell to the ground clear onto the other side of the field. I raced to the end of the field to pick them up, but I shot them farther than I thought possible because more than half of them were missing. They must have gone so high they stuck into a cloud. Yep, that's what happened all right. I know because they poked a hole in a cloud, and that was when I felt a rain drop. When I realized I had lost my brother's hunting arrows, fear filled my heart. I could really use a friend, I thought to myself. Just then Cupid arrived. She helped me see the humor in the whole situation so when Ben chewed me out it wasn't as bad as I thought. I had learned to focus my attention on how Cupid and I laughed hysterically about the arrow flying over St. Peter's head.

I wanted to invite Cupid to my birthday party, but it would have been a little confusing trying to explain her to everyone. Besides, Cupid wasn't ready for that. Cupid didn't know the day of her birthday, only the year, 1897. It would have been hard to explain that she didn't live in a house but rather on my wall in a picture frame watching over me through the night. Sometimes Cupid talked me through my fears.

> Cats in the night
> Hold me tight,
> Peeking in my windowpane;
> Oh, it's just the summer rain.
> Cat's in the night
> No more fright;
> I'll sleep well tonight.

"Well, good-night, Cupid, and thanks for watching over me tonight and protecting me from the darkness in my soul. Now I lay me down to sleep, I pray the Lord my soul to keep ..."

In my childhood I had many dolls, but Sally was my favorite because she had a personality like Cupid. When

Cupid wasn't around, Sally was there to comfort me. Sally had a fake ponytail made of rubber. She reminded me of a classmate who wore a ponytail who also had the name of Sally. Sally had a charismatic personality and was liked by everyone. I didn't have many friends so I pretended that Sally, my doll, was my classmate and friend. When I wanted adventure, I called upon Cupid; when I wanted the nurturing of a mother, I played house with Sally and Martha, my make-believe mother.

In my fantasy world I could escape the abusive talk, along with the incest from my family and live in another world in my mind. My brother Ben, who is ten years older than I, liked to play games under the covers. The games Ben played became hurtful and fearful. My sister Lynn, who was eight years older than I, abused me while I was in the bath tub and in my bedroom. Lynn, at one point, took her anger out by probing my vagina with knitting needles.

Cousins, an uncle, neighbors, and my brother-in-law all targeted me for sexual abuse. Sexual abuse is a broad statement as it can be anything from gestures, streaking in front of you, fondling and the list goes on. I once read that, "Sexual abuse is like a cancer, a cancer of the soul."[1] I can identify with that as the cancer of abuse spread out touching and affecting every relationship I ever encountered.

I believe that sexually abused individuals are crying out for help, crying out from the depth of their souls. I reached out by getting sound psychological and spiritual counseling and I have read many self-help books. I suggest reading books on self-image, emotions, relationships, addictions, and sexual behaviors. In the bibliography are some of the books that I found helpful. I believe that one of the most important tools in healing the traumatic experiences of abuse is building friendships with at least five trustworthy people, possibly join a support group. Journaling thoughts and feelings with pencil may also be helpful. We are more likely to be open and honest when writing in pencil as pencil erases, whereas pen is permanent. The scar of abuse need not be permanent if one will deal with the abuse and keep in focus that what happened was not his/her fault.

---

[1] Unknown as the source

# Chapter Two

# THE TRUTH WILL SET YOU FREE

As a young adult I took the philosophy, "Live for today without a care about tomorrow." However, that pattern of living was overturned when a phone call from the doctor's office informed me that my physical was abnormal. The nurse told me that I needed to check into the hospital for further tests. My so-called tough exterior was broken through by tears and prayers to spare my life because I had two children and a husband to look after. Brandy was only six years old and Ken was four. I pleaded with God to spare my life. I bargained with God about how I would change and try to get to know Him better. I had an endless list of do's and don'ts, as well as a sense of duty based religious sacrifices that I thought would appease God.

I had a simple D&C (Dilation and Curettage) to find the problem. After the surgery Dr. Jacobs was up front with me and told me how lucky I was to have come in when I did, for he had just saved my life. I had to stay an extra day to get the results back from the tests on the piece of tissue that he had removed which he thought was cancerous.

The test came back from the lab. "I can't understand it," Dr. Jacobs explained. "I saw it with my own eyes, but there is nothing there." I don't know if God healed me or allowed the doctor to see something that wasn't there. All I know is that I got a clean bill of health. Whatever it was, God did His part and now I had to fulfill my part of the bargain. I didn't realize at that time that one doesn't bargain with God.

Soon after my release from the hospital I got involved in a neighborhood Bible study. I needed a Bible, but I wasn't about to put good money out for one. I was told about the ministry of Gideons International that gave Bibles away. I inquired about these people and found one in my area.

I was soon knocking at the door of a Gideon member's home. Bob Davidson was not at home, but his wife Darlene was. She tried to give me a pocket-size Gideon New Testament Bible; however, I refused it, for I wanted a whole Bible. After my insistence and dire need for this book, she managed to give me one. The Gideons place Bibles in hotel rooms, and they had just replaced them in the nearby hotels. In the meantime, the discarded Bibles were dormant in Davidson's basement. I didn't care that it was a used one just as long as I had one to read, a whole one. I thanked Darlene and I left.

Three months later in October of 1975, I was convinced that Jesus was God's Son, sent to earth to be our Savior. I believed the stories I had been reading about his gruesome death and that he died for my sins, along with Jesus rising from the grave. His death on the cross and resurrection from the dead was my only way to eternal life. I sat with my Bible in hand in front of the flaming fire of our fireplace. I was mesmerized as I gazed into the flames, digesting what I had read from that poignant black book over the past few months. In the quietness of my heart I asked Jesus to come into my life as I confessed my sinful ways. At that moment I felt peace and warmth within me from the Spirit of God.

There was no room for doubt that God was with me. I knew that what happened to me was not just a religious experience but a personal relationship with God through His Son Jesus, and that the Spirit of God was my teacher. All the penance and religious acts I had done in the past to try to attain restitution for my sins were over. For the first time in my life I felt free of my past sins; I felt a completion about me. God was faithful, and within one year my spouse and children also invited Jesus into their lives to be their Savior.

The Bible captivated me. The Holy Spirit drew me to study and learn His Word. I enrolled in The Moody Bible Institute in Chicago. I finished the correspondence classes and graduated in 1978. I became involved at that time in a fundamentalist church and conference. I taught women's Bible studies, ran the youth group, and taught Sunday School. I wrote inspirational material for the Baptist General Conference Women's Groups in my area which I became president of, along with being a member on the Conference Women's Board. God became my whole life. God gave me self esteem as He taught me to accept myself as He accepted me. I was amazed to know that God knew everything about me and loved me just the same. Through this whole time I was careful to observe my daily quiet time.

As I read, studied and memorized verses from the Bible along with meditating over the verses, I came to know Jesus in a personal way. I heard the quiet whispers of love from the Savior filling my heart and penetrating my soul. The more I learned about Jesus, the more I wanted him to be Lord of my life. While I sought to know God's will and direction, I became convinced that I had to be truthful in all areas of my life, including my past. I started being truthful with my husband. I told Kenny about the deep inner secrets that I had concealed from him for many years. We experienced some distress in our marriage because it was difficult for Kenny to comprehend my honest openness with him about my past. At this point I didn't know if our marriage could stand the upheaval that the truth was causing. However, God promised me that "the truth would set me free." I stood by the faith that God would heal our marriage. Our marriage did survive and my love for Kenny grew as did his love for me. From that moment, I knew that nothing could ever stand between Kenny and me again. Our marriage took much hard work overcoming the codependent relationship to bring it to a healthy one.

Several years later I felt that nudge once again to get honest; this time I was to be straightforward with my adult children. For their sakes, so I thought, I had lived a deception about being pure to my wedding day. Now, Brandy and her husband were coming home for a visit. By the time they got to our home I was feeling more than a nudge; I felt an out right push to get all the truth out. I shared with Kenny the need to apologize to my grown children. Kenny seemed to think that by telling Brandy and Ken, I would destroy the relationship that Brandy and I had developed over time. However, I was more determined than ever to be honest, so I told him, "No. When you and I became honest with our past, it strengthened us. Truth will not hurt Brandy and Ken and it will set me free."

In the end, I shared the truth of my impure actions with Brandy. She was quiet at first. Then she started to cry. I asked her what her tears were all about. She looked up at me with tears streaming down over her checks and said, "Mom, you never experienced what I experienced on my wedding night." In the moments to follow we cried and grieved for the loss of my virginity. She later sent me this poem.

Today darkness and sorrow filled my heart
For what I once thought was truth fell apart.
The truth came out and so did the tears
Because the things that came out were my fears.

But instead of falling apart,
Love took control and ruled my heart.
For now instead of seeing a perfect one,
I see now a human, who is very strong.
The relationship we once had will never be
For the one we received today is honesty.
And the trust we now have shall never be broke.
Thank you for all you taught me and
Are teaching me on honesty, love, and relationships.

Your daughter and friend,
Brandy

The same weekend that Brandy was home, I was able to talk to my son Ken in the laundry room where I burst out with a summarized version of what I had told Brandy. I apologized to Ken while we were in the laundry room for what I had told him years prior, "If you ever sleep with someone, I expect you to marry her." Now I apologized to him for trying to dominate him to live by my biased way of thinking. I now was able to leave that judgment call between Ken and God. Ken did not respond to me in the laundry room. Spiritually, he backed off. To this day we have never discussed the matter. At this time the Lord was laying the foundation for me to understand both the power of truth and of freedom.

I believe what English reformer John Wycliffe once said; "in the end the truth will conquer." Truth was closing the door to self-defeat and at the same time opening an alternative door to self-esteem. The once felt shame of my past was replaced with integrity.

# Chapter Three

# The ABYSS

A few years later, my mom had a major setback as a result of a visit from her out-of-town sister. Aunt Maryann's arguments and words seemed to put Mom into a major depression. In desperation Dad telephoned me to inform me that Mom wouldn't get out of bed, even to go to the bathroom or to get up to eat. I went to my parent's home the next day and found Mom in a fetal position in bed. Mom hugged me and cried. With my help Mom was able to sit up, however, she wouldn't stand. I couldn't leave this frail human being home for Dad to take care of. In my opinion Mom seemed too have lost all hope. I called the hospital and social services to get some physical help for her, but nothing was available on such short notice. I only had one alternative, and that was to do my best to get Mom into my car and take her home where I could take care of her.

I packed my parents' clothes and toiletries, shut off all utilities and struggled to get Mom to the car. I thanked God for Ike, an elderly friend of ours, who came along with me for the ride. Ike and I virtually carried Mom to my car because she hadn't any strength or desire to walk. Her body odor was so appalling that we found it hard breathing on the way home.

Lee, my daughter-in-law, helped me to get Mom into my house and into the bathroom where she was able to urinate after being confined to her bed for several days. Then I gave Mom a sponge bath. I was gentle and loving as I handled her as if she were a priceless jewel. After all, she was my mom.

My mom and I were still in the bathroom when she started to cry in a childlike way. She looked up at me with her sky blue eyes, tattered and drawn, and said, "My dad, he was a good man, wasn't he?" I assured her that my grandfather had been good, even though, from the stories I had heard about him I didn't believe it, however, for right now Mom needed that comfort. The argument with her sister Maryann had been about the abuse inflicted on the family from their father. Maryann had provoked some memories and experiences that Mom had so desperately tried to block out. Mom didn't want to face the history of her past. In trying to push aside her feelings, Mom retreated within herself for weeks.

When Mom was recuperating in my home she shared many of her inner secrets about her family dynamics. As Mom shared, it sounded much like when I grew up with my siblings in similar abusive situations.

The next month or more I took care of Mom with much cuddling, attention, and love. We were bonding as we never had before. I was glad I was there for her. Mom was soon able to walk with her walker, along with the help from my son, my dad, my husband, and me. With Mom back on her feet, Mom, Dad, Kenny, and I started to talk about moving Mom and Dad back to their own home. Mom seemed to look forward to going to her homestead, and she agreed to move home in August sometime. However, before that time she had a heart attack.

The county nurse was at our house at the time the heart

attack was in progress. The nurse informed me of the situation with Mom's heart immediately after checking her.

I drove 80 mph or faster to get her to the hospital fifty miles away, praying as I drove. The hospital staff rushed her into a private area where the doctor examined her. The doctor called me aside and informed me that I had to be strong for my dad. He needed to be told that it looked like Mom wasn't going to pull through and would probably die from the massive heart attack. The doctor gave her a couple of days at the most to live.

"Be strong for dad," I thought. "I'm all alone." My mind raced about, I was about to lose my mother and this doctor expected me to be strong for dad. My legs felt like they were about to cave beneath me, my heart raced sporadically, my blood seemed to be sweltering inside.

In agony a cry from within me went out to God. I watched the doctor's lips moving as he explained the procedures that he was taking in an effort to ease my mom's passing. However, I never heard anything being said to me, as I was in deep distress from the thought of mom dying.

My friends called the church prayer chain and many were praying for my mother's recovery. God answered our prayers and He gave Mom the strength to fight for her life. I was able to take her to my home within two weeks.

One month after my mother's massive heart attack in my home Mom sat in the over-stuffed brown Lazy Boy rocker, wrapped in my son's baby blue and red nylon sleeping bag. Looking at her, I saw a ninety-nine pound, frail body of a depleted old woman. She looked ninety years old, although she hadn't yet reached seventy-five. I touched the tip of the spoon to my lips to check the temperature before feeding her.

"Open, Mom, it's ready. It's getting easier to turn you on the bed, to bathe you, now that I bought those big oversized fluffy towels to roll you up in. I will always be here to take care of you."

I tried to chit-chat with Mom to cover up the disquieting sensation within my abdomen. The agonizing, lingering inner pain of waiting for her to care for me was over. Instead, here I was, waiting on her, having to meet her every need, from feeding her to bathing her, and to put it bluntly, to wiping her butt.

It was an early spring morning. I had just finished cleaning up the stench in Mom's room from her secretions during the night. I hand rubbed and rinsed out the spotted areas in her tainted blue, faded, worn, sleeveless nightgown. I squirted some Era detergent on the spotted areas of the old white, stained, yellowing sheets, and then tossed them into the washer. I opened the window to give some freshness to the area now smelling of disinfectant and Lysol. Through the open window in Mom's bedroom, the refreshing gentle wind brought the fragrance of lilacs into the room overtaking the smell of disinfectants.

Oh, how the fragrance of lilacs filled my nostrils and hypnotized me for a time of pure pleasure! I was drawn to a place within myself as I gazed out the window over-looking the pasture and saw my chestnut Arab throwing his head as if he were inviting me to ride. He must have sensed me watching him because he looked up and whinnied.

"Oh, if only I could come out, Kojack."

A warm breeze blew the white percale, tied back curtains. With the breeze came the buzzing of a yellow jacket as it fluttered into the window, bringing my thoughts back to where I was this day and the sting of life I was about to feel in the moments to come.

Is she strong enough after the massive heart attack to probe her memory for the events which I somehow blocked out? Can I ask her? Will she be honest with me? I have so many questions in my apprehensive mind. I feel as if I am on a roller coaster ride that is hell-bound. There is no getting off. There is no turning around. I am so close to hell that I can practically taste the thickness of the sulfur in the air. I need to know the answer to a haunting question that probably only my mother can answer.

I stop to pray, "Dear God, please give me the answer."

I say, "Mom," as I kneel down at the chair that engulfs her hunched and curled little body. I run my fingers through her greasy, lifeless, graying hair. Her wrinkled tattered skin is silky soft like a baby's butt.

"Mom, I need to know, and I need you to be honest with me. You see, back in my memory, I remember telling you something about Ben." I hesitate for a split second, "But, but I don't remember what I told you. I only remember standing at Ben's bedroom door feeling so very alone, abandoned, rejected and crying because he told me I wasn't allowed to sleep with him anymore because I had told Mom. Mom, what did I tell you?"

I was still kneeling by her side. Then, slowly, she talked. I don't remember exactly what she said, but she did some mumbling, and I pressed her once again. She looked toward me. She hesitated, stared down and was off in a trance as if she were reliving the event of thirty-eight years ago. She had a look of shame on her face. She rubbed her crippled arthritic hands together nervously. She didn't look at me. She had her chin tucked to her neck like a turtle trying to hide within his shell. Then, slowly, hesitantly, she answered my question.

"You said, 'He monkeyed with you.'"

"What does that mean, Mom?"

She shook her head, "I don't know. You only said he was monkeying with you."

Being persistent, I continued to ask my mother why she hadn't done anything about it. I think I caught her off guard because her response was, "I didn't want to get my son in trouble."

A burst of emotions welled up inside me. Fury, anger

and rage overcame the past thirty-eight years of numbness like a typhoon loosened off the Mediterranean, but I tried to keep myself composed so I didn't upset my sick, frail mother. I saw her take a quick glimpse at me. I wasn't hiding my feelings very well. I'm sure she saw the hurt on my face, and for the first time I think I was able to identify my inner pain with hers. Only seconds had passed, but to us it was a life time of events swooping down upon us like a turkey vulture ready to devour the dead carcasses of yesterday. After her statement and her glimpse toward me, I sensed in her saddened sky blue eyes the shame of caring for her only son, not for her youngest daughter. Nervously, she tried to cover that feeling, and she quickly tried to rescue herself by stating, "And my daughter. I didn't want anything to happen to you."

Didn't she know? Didn't she understand? Didn't she realize that what took place thirty-five, forty years ago had set me up to be a victim of child abuse? It set me up for a continuous cycle of molestation from my brother, along with the on-going victimization from my oldest sister Lynn. Lynn's anger and rage toward me has continued throughout my life. Lynn was the most resentful, bitter, revengeful person that I had ever encountered. It seemed to me that throughout my childhood, teen years, and into my adult life, I was the one Lynn focused her vicious attacks upon. Lynn's devilish, conniving, cunning, scheming, malicious, and cruel ways were her way of getting even with me for something that I hadn't any idea I had done to her. I could never understand why she seemed to be misguided in her thinking that I not only took her daddy from her but her husband, too?

"What, Daddy? Did I say Daddy?" Memories came, flashbacks, then more memories. I had asked one question, not realizing that one answer would lead me down through a black hole, through the abyss of my childhood. No, Mom didn't understand. She didn't understand because Mom also was a victim of abuse.

Over the next couple months Mom was able to share many of her locked up emotions and feelings with me. Mom and I were able to share feelings of pain which we both experienced at the hand of older siblings. For the first time I was able to identify with Mom, which helped me to see how much we were really alike. We were both sensitive and, above all, we both hurt deeply from the abuse of others. History had repeated itself from Mom's generation to mine.

I remember in the late 1970's my sister Lynn, along with her spouse Louie, and three sons left the city of Minneapolis and moved in with Mom and Dad until they could find a house to live in. Dad gave Louie a job in the company Dad owned.

Lynn's living arrangements with my parents were short lived because Lynn and Mom got into an awful brawl. Lynn along with her family ended up at my door step where I took them in. After about three weeks of Louie constantly complaining about the bed, the food and whatever else came to his mind; Kenny informed me that they had to leave. After they found temporary housing, Dad gave Lynn and Louie some property to build a house on.

The property was in the same town where Kenny and I built our home. I was excited about my sister living close by. I yearned for us to finally be a family. However, it was short lived and Lynn was back to her old ways of jealousy and resentment. She took action to discredit me in every conceivable way possible.

Several friends of mine befriended Lynn because she was my sister. However, when Lynn started speaking badly about my character, my friends stood up for me. Lynn made havoc among many of my friends and acquaintances in our little community.

Lynn had joined the little Community Church that I attended. Soon a rumor came back to me that Lynn quit going to the church because of something that I had done to her. When I heard about the rumor, I went to Lynn and asked forgiveness. Forgiveness for something that I hadn't any idea of what I might have done for Lynn to be so revengeful toward me.

Lynn would not tell me what I did, but she insisted that she would never forgive me for as long as I lived. I went to our pastor and told him the problem. He went with me to Lynn's home to settle the problem and the rumor.

Lynn put on her religious pious act and said to the pastor, "Sam has done so much to hurt me, but I always forgive her. She knows that."

Lynn continued her pious act and told the pastor, "I was so glad when Sam found God because she was so mixed up in sex and drinking that I was worried about her."

Lynn was painting a pretty grim picture about me and I agreed with Lynn. "You're right, Lynn, I was bound for hell. However, I haven't any shame or guilt anymore because the blood of Jesus has wiped away my sins, and according to the Bible I am a new person in the power, and blood of Christ. By the way, Lynn, when did you ask Jesus into your life?"

"I've always been a good person and believed in God, not anything like you."

My reply was, "You're right, Lynn. The Bible tells me that my righteousness is that of a filthy rag. I am in total agreement with God and you."

Lynn was lost for words because I would not let her words affect my walk with God. The pastor once again asked Lynn if she held any grudges against me or the church.

"Like I said, Pastor, Sam needed the church and I am glad that she changed her drug and alcoholic life style," Lynn replied. "I have always forgiven her for what she did."

Lynn was getting cruel with her remarks toward me. I wasn't about to agree to the last attacks on my character nor would I give her an argument which Lynn would find reason to hold against me.

Pastor looked at me and said, "Well, I guess if Lynn states she doesn't hold any grudges against you, we can leave here, for everything is settled according to Lynn."

Lynn never returned to the church and because she wasn't an active member her membership was abolished. The rumors Lynn started soon vanished. Everything in my church and community went back to normal. Most people forgot that Lynn was my sister.

Lynn got behind in her bank payments on the loan she had on the house she and Louie had built with my dad's help. Along with the house, Lynn lost the property that Dad gave her. Dad, being a business man, had some associates in another area several counties away where he got Louie a job. Lynn and Louie relocated to that area.

Lynn has an obsessive compulsion to evoke her misery on others. I would not argue with Lynn or give her any feedback to fuel an argument. Lynn then turned her revengeful and conniving spitefulness to my parents.

In the early 1980's Lynn wrote a very vindictive letter to Mom and Dad. In the letter she told them that as far as she was concerned, they were no longer her parents. She accused them of abusing her. She also tried to play on Dad's subconscious with accusations that he believed Mom's "lies". What Lynn meant by 'lies,' I really don't know. From my own experience with Lynn's accusations against me, I think when Lynn talked about lies in her letter, this was just another one of Lynn's psychotic ways of thinking. Lynn sent a copy of the letter to her siblings. I think Lynn sent the letter hoping that someone would rescue her from the evil parents that she had been portraying in her sick mind, however, nobody rescued her.

Mom tried a number of times to ask Lynn to forgive her. After numerous attempts, Mom gave up and became bitter and angry over Lynn's vindictiveness toward her.

Several years went by with Mom still trying to appease Lynn and to get her forgiveness.

My mom's closest sister died and Mom telephoned Lynn for support, "Lynn, Aunt Fran died. Please come home. I need you."

Lynn was cruel when she answered Mom, "Well, I don't need you. As far as I'm concerned you can just drop dead!"

Mom grieved the loss of her beloved sister. At the same time Mom grieved over Aunt Fran, she experienced anger and bitterness over Lynn's cruel remarks to her on the telephone. Mom told me, "If that's the way Lynn wants to be, then she is dead in my eyes."

At Mom's house I noticed Lynn's graduation picture was missing from the place that it had hung on the wall. When I inquired about the picture, Mom said, "I was so angry at that piss-ant Lynn for not being there for me when Aunt Fran died, I took every picture of Lynn that I had, and I ripped every picture in little pieces, than I burnt them in an ashtray."

Every chance Lynn had, she became vicious toward our mother. Mom's void, from the absence of her oldest daughter, was filled by Mom being preoccupied with my children. I spent a lot of time with Mom while Lynn wasn't a part of Mom's or my life. Mom became real like the story of *Velveteen Rabbit.*

Together Mom and I worked at getting close in our relationship. We learned to trust each other. The love Mom and I shared was a great blessing to both of us. No one can ever steal the loving memories we built during the ten year period that Lynn choose not to be a part of us.

One day Lynn's oldest son, Dale went to my parents home and asked Grandpa and Grandma to please apologize again to his mother Lynn. My parents did go to Lynn's home at the request of Dale. When one takes responsibility of another's actions they share in the malfunction of a co-dependent relationship. Once again, Lynn was the controller in this co-dependent family's dynamics.

Lynn did reconcile with my parents when Mom and Dad arrived at her home. After the reconciliation, my parents spoke to Lynn on occasions. However, Mom and Dad were careful not to get too close or to trust her. Lynn stopped her feuding with Mom and Dad, however, once again Lynn chose me to be her victim.

While Mom was recuperating in my home after her heart attack, Mom called Lynn, "Hello, Lynn, I was just calling because I haven't heard from you for awhile."

Lynn responded, "Well, I won't call you while you're at Sam's house, so you'll have to call me."

I wondered if Lynn's verbal reprehensible attack was to punish me or to get our mother to take sides. One never knew what Lynn's true motives were. I don't think even Lynn knew. Lynn just had to be angry at someone along her pathway, might as well be Sam.

Mom recovered fairly rapidly from her heart attack in May. The middle of November Mom and Dad returned to their home. Taking care of my parents was rewarding, but at the same time it was difficult and draining both emotionally and physically.

When Mom and Dad returned to their own home, I felt that I had my home, my sanctuary back. I was joyful and content as I went about my household duties, caring for my children and spouse. However, into my tranquil, peaceful life, surfacing up through my subconscious, unwarranted images invaded my thought patterns. Before I knew it, I was facing the malady that I had blocked out all those years, the affliction of sexual abuse.

As I faced the amnesia of my childhood, I discovered several perpetrators that started on me when I was six and that the sexual abuse had continued through my teen years. One of my family members impregnated me when I was twelve. I was not aware of the pregnancy because my mom took me for an abortion shortly after my thirteenth birthday.

The flashbacks about the sexual abuse came and went in the matter of three months. However, I had emotional work to do. I had to face the memories, the experiences, and the feelings that went with the flashbacks. When I was being abused as a child I had learned to evade my feelings by escaping into a pretend world with Cupid, Captain Novak, Sally, and Martha. In my adult world I learned to push aside the feelings and memories by becoming too busy, or with food, anger and control to name a few.

# Chapter Four

# I WAS SLOWLY DYING

Mom was very sentimental. Mom saved everything of mine from my first tooth to the locks of my golden hair. The heirlooms of my childhood were in an old cigar box with my favorite yellow ribbon tied to secure the treasures of my youth.

Mom handed me the box, "I thought you would like these. I even have your first bonnet in there."

"Mom, you saved this all those years, for what?"

"For you, I saved the little mementos, just for you." Tears welled up in Mom's eyes as she went on. "You were so small and tiny. You were my precious baby. You'll always be my baby, even though you're past forty-five. I want you to have these jewels of memories that I hold so dear to my heart."

I tried to be enthusiastic over Mom's box of junk. "Gee, thanks, Mom. They will be a treasure I will hand down to Brandy when she has a child." I chuckled to myself.

Several months later I ran across the cigar box in my closet. I took the box out of hiding and opened it to see exactly what was in the box. My eyes focused on my fifth grade report card. According to my report card I was ten years of age and my weight was only thirty-five pounds. As I gazed at the report card, memories flooded my inner being with feelings of dreaded fear and pain.

A flashback swooped upon me like the darkness inside a grave. The chasm of my past slowly opened to the deadness of my childhood. I curled up on the floor of my closet as I relived another hellish nightmare.

As a child I didn't have a room of my own; I had to share with Lynn. I was both physically and mentally abused by her. I wanted to share a room with the one I loved and trusted the most, but Ben rejected me because I told. I decided the closet like little room in the back used for junk collecting would be my hiding place. I cleaned out the closet for myself. I moved my private possessions along with my dolls into the closet.

I was playing house when Ben came into my territory, the closet. It was there where Ben tied my hands together with a rope and anchored the rope to the clothes rod in the closet. I whispered a prayer but no one heard. I concluded there wasn't a God; if there was one, he would have heard my silent screams within. I alone would have to carry the secrets in my soul. Ben then took off his belt and tightened the belt around my neck until I felt faint and ready to pass out. Ben warned me if I ever told about our secrets again he would kill me.

Grandma Lindsky, an old Polish woman who lived down the street from us was beaten by her daughter-in-law, Edith. Edith, in a drunken stupor, came for Mom's help after she brutally beat Grandma. Mom and I went to help Grandma. Grandma was a bloody mess with both eyes blackened, along with contusions all over Grandma's body. Grandma's bib-apron made from the material of a flour sack and dilapidated purple flowered dress with graying white lace were torn to pieces, hanging with threads from Grandma's body.

Grandma was moved to a nursing home where she died, having never recovered from the beating.

Ben used Grandma's death to implant fear into me so that I wouldn't tell the secrecy of what went on between us. Ben would pick me up by the head with the rest of me dangling and then he would carry me to wherever he was going to abuse me. When Ben was finished with me he would ask me if I wanted to see Grandma. I knew exactly what he meant. Grandma was beaten, Grandma was moved, and then Grandma died.

Around the same time that Ben was abusing me, Dad started to fondle me. My dog Jimmy tried to attack my dad when Dad tried to have intercourse with me. Dad grabbed the little Cocker Spaniel and snapped Jimmy's neck, killing him instantly. Dad threw the dog to the floor. Dad finished his sexual attacks on me; he got up from my bed and picked Jimmy up. I watched Dad through the upstairs bedroom window bury my dog in the field next to our house. I never shed a tear for I learned to be numb to any feelings.

I couldn't tell Mom what Ben and Dad had done to me so I would tell her about my stomach ache. Mom thought I was constipated so she gave me enemas several times throughout the week. I fought Mom the last time she tried to give me an enema so Dad came into the bathroom to give me the enema. That was the last time I told Mom that my tummy hurt.

At dinner time we all sat at the table. Ben sat to my left and Dad sat to my right. Just seeing Ben and Dad made my stomach queasy. I soon started to vomit at every meal. I couldn't eat or I would get sick, yet Dad insisted that I eat. The last time Dad insisted that I eat I vomited right into my plate at the table. Mom sided with me and didn't make me eat. Mom said that I would eat when I got hungry. I tried to eat but I would vomit everything that went in me.

Mom took me for a physical check up because I was

losing weight rapidly. The doctor examined me and told Mom that my tonsils were rotting and poisoning my system. The doctor thought that I had a severe case of tonsillitis. Little did the doctor know that my tonsils were rotting from stomach gases because of my daily vomiting. I was slowly dying from being anorexic at only ten years of age.

After recalling the memories through my flashbacks, I then felt a need to confront every one of the perpetrators either in person or by letter.

# Chapter Five

# TAKING MY LIFE BACK

My life was again interrupted when Mom suffered her second heart attack during the first week of February, 1992.

After the heart attack I telephoned my siblings to come to the hospital. Lynn, the first to arrive at the hospital, came with an attitude of nastiness toward me.

I cornered Lynn in the hospital lounge area to tell her bluntly that I would not allow her to upset Mom and that she had to pull her act together and be an adult in Mom's presence.

From past experience, I knew Lynn wouldn't give up her resentful and unbearable ways and that I would be her target for revenge. I was right and at every opportunity Lynn made direct and intimidating remarks toward my family or me. Lynn was exasperated when I didn't respond to her feeble attacks geared toward me.

Mom was transferred to a second hospital for immediate surgery after she suffered a third heart attack. In the dawn of that morning Kenny and I left for the second hospital traveling at the phenomenal speed of 90 mph. We arrived at the hospital within an hour. I ran to Mom's room just as they put her into the elevator to take her to surgery. I went with Mom to the surgical room holding her hand and telling her how much I loved her.

Mom was always afraid of death. However, at this time she looked up at me, with peace in her eyes and said, "I'm not afraid to die." I kissed her and went to the waiting room to wait with the rest of my family.

I needed to confront Ben about the incest. I think he knew what was on my mind because he avoided being alone with me. However, at one point I caught his arm in the hospital corridor.

"Ben, I remember what you did to me, and I don't hold it against you." He thanked me and gave me a hug. I then asked him if it was Billy, an old man who ran the gas station in our little town, who abused him. Ben quickly answered, "No."

Later that evening Mom was out of surgery and in the intensive care unit. I was with her when Ben walked in with his spouse Kate. I moved aside so that he could get past me to Mom's bedside. Ben at that point grabbed my clothes at the neck and holding my clothes in his grip said, "It was Billy, but that's our secret."

Louie, Lynn's spouse was at the hospital much of the time also. Louie was a constant reminder to me of his cunning, seductive ability, which he used to seduce me in my teen years.

In the summer of 1962 I went to Minneapolis to babysit for Lynn and Louie while they both worked. At that time they had two boys of preschool age.

Lynn and Louie verbally fought a lot during my stay with them. At one point their fights became physical. Lynn and Louie were throwing punches at each other. Lynn's glasses went flying as he slapped her and with the impact of his hand she fell back, landing on the floor. I had seen enough and stepped between them. I yelled at Louie and told him never to hit my sister again. Louie looked sheepish when I yelled at him; then turned and walked out the door.

Evidently Louie couldn't handle me interrupting his attacks on Lynn. I humiliated and discredited him in his codependent power of control over Lynn. Little did I know I would pay the consequence for stepping in to protect Lynn.

I learned in my adult life that there is a pattern to most abusers' strategy, details and variations may differ and not all abusers follow the pattern in the full extent. For the most part sexual abuse doesn't just happen; it is organized and consciously planned out. These plans could take place in the matter of minutes, or planned out over days, months and even years depending on the cunningness of the abuser.

Dr. Dan B. Allender in his book *The Wounded Heart* writes about four stages that a perpetrator plans and organizes to set up a victim for sexual abuse. In stage one, the perpetrator purposefully sets into motion a relationship with his/her victim. With the relationship special gifts, privileges, and or treatments are bestowed to the victim that requires secrecy between the victim and the abuser. Along with the relationship comes an intimate bonding held together with more secretiveness which in turn sets up the next stage.

Stage number two involves physically touching of the victim, that seems appropriate but in a demeaning way; however, in actuality it is inappropriate touching which confuses the victim, especially if he/she is young and trusting.

In stage number three the relationship between the abuser and the victim is sabotaged. The terror of the betrayal is inconceivable as the victim feels powerless and perplexed. Mixed emotions over the ecstasy of the relationship and contempt for the actions the perpetrator takes control of the victim's body and soul.

In the fourth stage he/she instills fear and loyalty through threats of violence toward the one being sexually assaulted or against other family members, friends, pets or even toys if the victim is very young. A continuance of intimidation to keep the secrecy is rigorously planted within the victim's mind. The perpetrator's intention is to take away all power that the victim may have and in the process "destroy the body and soul" if their victim tells.[2]

Minneapolis was extremely hot and humid especially on the second floor of the diminutive apartment where my sister and her family lived in mid-summer of 1962. Before sending the boys off to bed, I would cool Lynn's boys off in a tub of water. The boys weren't completely potty trained and sometimes had an accidental bowel movement in the bathtub. I would just clean it up and fill the tub back up with water. Louie came home and witnessed the boys' accident in the tub. He was furious with the boys, not knowing which one had the bowel movement, he pulled his belt from his pants and whipped the bare butts of both of the boys and threw them into their bed. I tried to console the boys; Louie yelled at me for making them into crybabies. Louie did things to intimidate me and put the fear of Louie in me.

I was sitting in the unventilated, stuffy upstairs apartment in Minneapolis in my summer shorty pajamas reading a book. I heard Louie at the top of the stairs; I started for the bedroom that I shared with the boys. Before I got to the bedroom door Louie entered the apartment, he asked me where I was going. I answered to get my night robe. Louie convinced me that it would be all right to cool off in my baby doll pajamas. That night Louie kissed me on the cheek as I headed for bed. I felt a little uneasy but blew it off as nothing.

Little did I know that was the beginning of stage number two of a perpetrator. Louie followed through with the rest of the stages that a perpetrator goes through seducing me. Louie worked on my emotions by telling me of the pain Lynn would have to go through if I told. He continued to lay guilt on me of how it was my entire fault when I sat in my sexy pajamas night after night. Louie was good at making me feel guilt for how I hurt my sister. At the same time Louie continued to have sexual contact with me.

The guilt trip induced by Louie was more than I could handle. I began to have nightmares of the abuse I had encountered when I was six, or was I eight? I'm not really sure for somewhere through my childhood of abuse I blocked out two years of time. In my nightmares, I started to talk in my sleep revealing the sex Louie was having with me.

Lynn overheard me talking in my sleep. When she confronted me in the morning, I told about Louie's sexual involvement with me. Louie was very convincing when he told me it was my entire fault so in telling Lynn the details I took full responsibility for the adulterous act.

I didn't realize that through the years Louie was still victimizing me. I only knew my perceptiveness indicated something was wrong. The way he would touch my arm or squeeze my shoulder made my skin crawl. Louie would make sure Lynn saw him touching me. Once he stated to my mother that he married the wrong daughter. That statement kept me as far away from him as possible.

Louie and Lynn's relationship never did improve; they continued to bicker and fought on into the 1970's when they lived in the same area we did. Louie would go to the bar or tavern in our town until closing time; then he would phone our house and come over at two o'clock in the morning. He would rant and rave about how he had to live with such a cruel and vindictive individual, meaning my sister. Several times Louie would beg us to take his oldest son before Lynn completely destroyed him. I never knew what Louie was referring to and deep down inside I was afraid to find out. Kenny and I would sober him up, pray with him, and around five or six in the early morning he would leave for home.

The last time we sobered Louie up, prayed with him and sent him off, Louie went to the house of one my girl friends at the crack of dawn, knowing that her husband had just left for work, and asked her for sexual favors. I was angry when I found out what Louie did to Julie, my girlfriend. From that point on when Louie called I told him to go home. He soon got the message and quit calling.

After rehashing in my mind the past thirty years starting with the Minneapolis episode of abuse, I decided to take my life and my power back from Louie and wrote him a letter. I looked for the perfect moment to hand it to him. I was now stalking the perpetrator. It was my move and I held the knowledge and power inside myself in the presence of a perpetrator. I handed Louie the letter in the corridors of the hospital. As I handed him that letter, I felt powerful and a piece of my life seemed to fall into order.

After handing the letter to Louie, he avoided the hospital for several days. When he did come back, he avoided me revealing to other members of my family Louie's guilt of victimizing me over the years.

Every day for weeks I drove to the hospital. On weekends Kenny, my children, and I lived in a motel room close to the hospital.

I would spend hours at the hospital talking to Mom. I hugged her, and at times she would squeeze my hand. We had very little response from her. She seemed to respond to my dad's voice sporadically. Dad sat for hours just holding her hand. Once in a while I would see her eyes open and she would move her fingers in Dad's hand. I would fluff her pillow and talk so gently to her. I would tell her how much I loved her and I would remind her that she was a good mom.

Lynn would try to acknowledge her presence to Mom and would repeat, "It's me Mom, Lynn. I am here, too." However, Lynn's voice was so abrasive and coarse that I once asked her to please try to talk more gently to Mom. She didn't like it and continued trying to be in competition with me.

---

2 Material and ideas taken from *The Wounded Heart* by Dr. Dan B. Allender; Foreword by Dr. Larry Crabb

# Chapter Six

# THE ANNIVERSARY

Mom and Dad were celebrating their fiftieth anniversary while Mom was in the hospital. In honor of my parents' anniversary, I made them an elaborate cake. I called upon friends to celebrate this big event with us at the hospital. My friends knew they weren't there to celebrate my folks' anniversary, but rather they were there to give me moral support, in opposition to my sister's verbal abuse vented toward me. Whenever outsiders were present, Lynn acted nicely, which gave me some moments to relax in her presence.

On the way to the hospital, Kenny and I stopped at a K-Mart store to buy a knife to cut the cake. In Mom's hospital room I took the shiny knife out of the package, and as I did, it was like I was moving in slow motion because I was having a flashback. I recalled hiding a knife under my pillow as a child to stop someone from abusing me.

The flashback was one I had had before. The flashback was about Lynn probing my vagina with her little pink knitting needles. This time the flashback contained more information; this time I was recalling why Lynn probed me with the knitting needles. Lynn was being raped by a mentally challenged overgrown boy who was around Ben's age; we called him Big Jack. Big Jack hung around our house; everyone teased him that he had a crush on Lynn. Lynn screamed to me for help; however, I blocked it out and went merrily on my way for I thought rape was normal; after all it happened to me quite a lot. However, Lynn was furious with me for not getting her some help.

Lynn was on one side of Mom's bed and I on the other when Lynn stated with a hint of sarcasm in her voice, "We need to be a family." She was looking at my friend Barb when she said this. I knew from the sound of her voice and her eyes on my friend that her statement was not genuine.

My sarcastic response to Lynn was, "We were never a family! So why start now?" I continued, "By the way, Lynn, do you still have those knitting needles you used on me?"

Lynn was very nervous and responded quickly with her speech becoming fast as if the past was haunting her. She said, "I have lots of knitting needles; I knit all the time."

"No, Lynn I am talking about the little pink ones which you prodded and raped me with. By the way, do you remember what Big Jack did to you? Well, that is exactly how I felt when Louie touched me."

"Big Jack didn't rape me!"

"Oh, did I say he raped you?"

Some of the nursing staff and other friends and family started to come into the room. Lynn quickly gathered herself and put on her nice side once again. I passed the cake around; I felt a sense of power with the knife in my hand.

Nothing had been resolved in Lynn's and my relationship or between her abusive husband and me. Yet, I believe for Ben's sake Lynn tried desperately to pretend we were a family. Lynn did whatever it took to get Ben's approval even if it meant denying her true feelings.

It was a frigid, frosty February morning when Kenny

and I drove to the hospital to celebrate my parent's anniversary. Kenny always liked the radio playing but today he shut the radio off. He was quiet at first, then gradually but guardedly he started to share the depth of his inner most thoughts. Kenny talked and I listened; after all he had been listening to my stories over the past couple of months. The least I could do was hear him out.

Kenny was reminiscing over the names I shared with him some twenty years ago when I got honest with Kenny over my relationships. Kenny was bringing to surface every incident I poured my heart out to him.

Why was Kenny doing this to me? I felt myself getting furious over Kenny rehashing old events. However, I kept my cool and sat and listened when I realized Kenny was putting this nightmare of mine together for himself. I then relaxed a bit and let him continue.

When Kenny and I left the hospital Kenny started all over recalling the guys I had sex with including Louie, with whom I believed at one time that it was my fault for the sex we shared. Kenny harped on this the whole ninety miles home.

I had no idea where Kenny was going with this informative conversation. Kenny pulled the car up in our driveway. I said, "Let's go in and finish this conversation inside."

"No," Kenny responded. "It was in the car that we first had sex, and it is in the car where I want to apologize for victimizing you also. I am truly sorry; will you ever forgive me for taking advantage of you like the others?"

Kenny and I both cried and together we forgave one another. Kenny then asked if we could renew our wedding vows. Kenny bowed his head and in prayer asked God for His forgiveness of his sexual conduct before we were married. Kenny and I followed with vows to each other. In Kenny's and my heart, we celebrated our wedding day on my parents' anniversary. Kenny doesn't recall the date of this event, however every February 26 I reminisce that moment in my heart and how much his love means to me.

Over the years Kenny's commitment to my good taught me self-acceptance. I learned from Kenny how to establish boundaries in our relationship. He taught me the difference between sex and love. When I was honest with Kenny years ago, Kenny told me that his lovemaking is the ultimate expression of his love for me. We have never had sex from this time forth, however, we have had caressing and passionate lovemaking, which is my ultimate response to my husband.

# Chapter Seven

# BREANN

I was nearing forty-six years of age; it was time for my yearly pap smear and physical. The nurse took me into the examination room, and handed me a gown to change into. I was sobbing endlessly as Dr. Jacobs entered the examination room with me. "I can't let you do it! I can't let you examine me and I don't know why."

The good doctor reassured me that he wouldn't examine me; I was to make another appointment when I was ready. However, Dr. Jacobs seemed puzzled with my hysteria because this was unusual for me to lose control. He held me close and consoled me as my tears ran down my face and onto his freshly starched white lab coat. I was reminded of the Psalm 54:4 where God acknowledges my tears and places them in a bottle. I was encouraged by the words of the Psalm running through my mind as I put aside the fear and dreaded feeling within. I composed myself, got dressed, and left for home.

Through the next week pieces of flashbacks kept intruding into my somewhat serene life. They brought haunting little bits of painful events. I was once again experiencing shortness of breath and panic attacks until finally the whole picture from the flashbacks came into focus. The flashbacks contained a picture of me around thirty years earlier. I was a small framed child of ninety pounds with vivid blue eyes and messy long blonde hair standing in the doorway of the kitchen. With my chin tucked in toward my chest and my shamefaced eyes focused on the floor, I mumbled my inner pain to my mother's half-listening ears, "He did it again, Daddy did it again." Then I turned and went back to my lonely place in the attic of our apartment building to finish coloring.

My thirteenth birthday came and went. September was rounding the corner and school would soon be starting. I hadn't any enthusiasm or drive to go on. Mom took me to the doctor, who examined me. There was much talking in the outer room between my mom and the doctor. The doctor returned, ordered me to put my legs up in the stirrups and began to scold me as he reached into my vagina with a spoon and claw like tools. I held back the tears so not to let him know he was hurting me. At that moment the gentle soft little girl changed into a bitter, cold, and distant creature. I hated my life and all that it stood for. I realized that if I were to make it in this cruel world, I would have to go it alone, for there wasn't anyone whom I could trust, not even my mother. While the doctor pulled and pushed with his tools in my vagina, he also put force on my stomach with his oversized hand. The pain was so excruciating that I just blocked it all out. In my mind, I thought of myself walking along the school fence, kicking up the autumn leaves under my feet. I came back from my trance just as the doctor was taking off his white gloves that were blood stained. The doctor added insult to the injury by saying, "You shouldn't be acting like a little tramp and doing such bad things to your parents." I wondered "what bad things" and most of all "what is a tramp?"

The cramping pain from within my uterus continued

throughout that day with a mass of bloody tissues plummeting from my womb and into the toilet. At one point I saw tears in my mother's eyes, but as usual she denied the tears or any feelings.

"The deepest pain was not physical; it was the agony of being betrayed by someone she loved. In many sexual traumas, the key issue is the betrayal of love and trust."[3]

My mind reflected back to the doctor calling me a tramp. There was a girl in the neighborhood that my parents called a tramp. My mom and dad had forbidden me to see her. I would sneak over to visit with Kathy; I observed every detail about her and listened to her obnoxious stories about her many boyfriends. I finally came to think that a tramp was a liar because of the ambiguous stories Kathy told. I then confirmed that I was a tramp because I was a liar, according to daddy's statements about me. To quote Dad, "A liar and a thief are lower than a snake's belly." I was well along in my adult life before I came to believe the shocking news that my dad could lie.

I was sitting at my computer when the flashbacks were forming in my mind; I typed them out, careful not to miss any details.

A flare of emotion subdued me as rage came up from the pit of my stomach like a volcano erupting. I felt the sting of an abortion detonate inside of me as I faced the darkness of my soul and the tomb of my baby.

Kenny, my spouse knew of some of the flashbacks that had been surfacing, so it wasn't a total surprise to him to hear and feel with me the outrageous torpedo that had just exploded in my body of memories. I sat at his feet and sobbed my story out. Then the sobs turned to rage as I grabbed hold of his jogging pants and tugged.

"How could they do this to me? How could they treat me this way? I was their daughter. For God's sakes, what did they do to me?"

It was at that moment that the LORD reached down to me and started the healing process. I questioned whether what I felt and believed about my mother taking me for an abortion was true, and I needed some sort of confirmation. Monty's name came to my thoughts. I met Monty several times at Women's Retreats. I knew that she worked with girls thinking about having an abortion, so I called her. Monty listened to my story as I choked through the details, describing what I remembered. Upon finishing my recollection, Monty sadly informed me that I had described an abortion of thirty some years ago. Monty was tender and compassionate to me. At that point, I knew God had Monty and my paths cross so that He could show me His tenderness and understanding through her. God understood my grieving, for He too lost a child through the depravity of mankind. I felt His presence as I hung up the phone.

My grieving process continued as I felt the pain of the loss of my childhood along with the death by abortion of my unborn child. I prayed and shared my hurtful memories with Kenny and several close friends. They caressed me when I needed caressing and listened when I needed to talk. They were there for me. The wall I put up around me began to be torn down by friendship and love. From behind the bitterness and harshness emerged the soft, tender, loving creature that God intended me to be. I had found me!

I wanted to confront the doctor who had performed this mutilation of my baby, Breann. I had talked to my mother years ago about how that doctor hurt me and how I had wanted to face him with the pain he had caused me, both physically and emotionally. Mom insisted that the doctor was dead. Mom said he had died of old age, however, I remember him being younger than my parents. I now understand why she wanted me to believe he was dead. She didn't want me to know that she was the one who had executed that resolution to kill my baby through the abortion. I needed to know if the doctor was really dead or if it was another cover up to protect me from the truth. A girl's name that lived in the apartment complex when all this supposedly happened came to mind. I checked information and got a phone number of the girl in the apartment where I had lived. To my surprise, Barbie had worked as a receptionist for the doctor in question and she gave me his address. Coincidental? I don't think so.

Six months later, the bitterness that I felt for the doctor was resolved and I came to forgive him. Following the six months of grieving and healing that I went through over the abortion of my baby, whom I named Breann, I felt a nudge inside to write to the doctor. I felt the need to pray earnestly before writing my letter.

The letter consisted of what I believed to be an abortion and the fact of it being from incest. I did not make any accusations toward the doctor; I only conveyed my beliefs and asked for truth.

I never received an answer, nor did I expect one. However, I still pray for the doctor in hope that he will someday come to the truth that abortions kill the innocent and make victims out of the mother of the child. I know because I was one of those victims. I never realized that I had had an abortion, but the abortion still robbed me of a tranquil life. Like many, I denied the effect of an abortion, but looking back, the results of the abortion on that grisly frigid autumn morning in the year of 1959 in the doctor's chambers changed my whole future.

My mother was still in the intensive care unit at the hospital when I got in touch with the memories of the abortion. I needed to share my memories with Mom even if she couldn't respond to me. Standing at Mom's bedside at the hospital, I sobbed out my pain to my mother as I told her of my experience of getting in touch with the physical and emotional pain of the abuse and the abortion. Kenny was next to me praying as I talked to Mom. I noticed a trickle of tears rolling down her check. I reached for Mom's hand and at that moment I felt Mom's thumb rub the back of my hand.

I believe that Mom heard me. I believe that Mom knew exactly what I was feeling. I felt in my heart that Mom understood my pain; I believe she felt the pain with me. I only wish we could have talked about the abuse that I had encountered. I wish that Mom and I could have healed together the abuse of my past and the part Mom played as a victim. However, I found comfort in that moment I shared with Mom. I reassured her that I forgave her, and that I would be all right as I processed the healing in my soul.

It had become emotionally draining for me as I drove daily the ninety mile stretch to see my mom in the hospital. Recalling the flashbacks from the abortion and other abusive situations was just too much for my psyche to handle, especially when I was trying to be polite to Dad, knowing that he had sexually abused me.

In desperation to keep my sanity I made several appointments with the psychologist on staff at the hospital. I would go and see Mom and Dad for an hour, go see the doctor, and then head home to ponder the events of the day.

Kenny was having a hard time watching me go through such trauma and decided to intervene for me. He felt he had to protect my honor and informed me that he was going to confront my dad about the abuse. There was no talking Kenny out of it, so I decided to go with Kenny to confront my dad.

Sunday afternoon Kenny and I went to my parents' home. It seemed so empty without Mom there. Kenny pulled a chair up next to my dad where he was sitting in the living room. Kenny was so very gentle with my dad. I could see Kenny had carefully thought out his words before speaking them. Kenny related the abuse that Dad had done. He said my heart had been broken and the need for it to be fixed was like Mom's when she had the heart surgery. "No, sir," my dad said, "I didn't do such a thing."

Many times in the past years Dad spoke of the abusiveness of a stepmother that he had when he was a young teen; and for some reason I believed at that moment that he was sexually abused by her.

My dad was resting his feet on a footstool. I moved closer to this gruffy old man and sat next to his feet on the footstool. "Dad, do you remember how humiliated you felt; how ashamed you were, and how frightened and embarrassed you were when your stepmother did that to you? Well, that's how I felt when you touched me."

Silence filled the room as Dad rubbed the top of his forehead with a back and forth motion over his brow. The silence was broken as Dad spoke with tears in his eyes he said, "I never wanted to hurt my girls."

For a swift moment Dad confessed to girls, plural, so he had also abused my sister according to his word. Caught off guard, he quickly resumed the position of a tyrant and once again went back to, "No, sir, I didn't do that."

There wasn't any point in pursuing the issue any further. Kenny and I headed back to our home. I did find some relief in the short-lived confession.

---

[3] Page 176, *Healing of Memories* by David A. Seamands

# Chapter Eight

# THE RED ROSE

Mom was still in Intensive Care, going into her ninth week. Each day she became more and more like a vegetable. I held on to hope the best I could. During this time I tried desperately to get my father to be accountable for his misdemeanors toward his girls. I even lowered myself to his standard and used his words that were so often spoken to me when I was growing up. "Dad do you remember telling me when I was young that 'a liar and a thief are lower than a snake's belly'? Dad, you robbed me and lied when you tried to cover up what you have done to me; however, you do have forgiveness in Jesus. But I can't forgive you Dad, until you ask."

My situation with Dad was as hopeless as Mom getting better. Dad was now leaning on Lynn to take care of him. It was heartrending because I thought my relationship with Dad over the past twenty years was mutual trust. Now Dad stayed clear of me when he could.

Mom lingered on into the eleventh week. Something had to be done. A meeting was called with the hospital staff, my dad, my sister, and me. Arrangements had to be made to have my mom put into an adult care facility. Dad was so angry at me for bringing it up. I took to the hospital the papers that my mom had signed leaving me the sole administrator for her care; I also gave the hospital the papers showing that Mom did not want to prolong her life.

Lynn was goading Dad on about me making these decisions when it wasn't for me to make. Lynn claimed that should be Dad's responsibility, not mine. My dad was old and fatigued from the eleven weeks of trying to hold on and wasn't thinking straight. However, he insisted Lynn take over.

The hospital staff had had enough of Lynn and her accusations against them for improper care and took advantage of the situation and put Lynn in her place. The head nurse said, "I'm sorry, but these papers are all legal and in order. We will have to comply with the legal documents here."

I left the room to say a final good-bye to my mother. Lynn and Dad followed. I asked Dad to walk me to the elevator. I confronted him once again. I noticed Lynn was lurking around the corner of the corridor listening to every word being said. When the elevator door opened, I reached my hand out to my father and said, "This is good-bye Dad, I can't be a part of you if you can't be honest with me." I turned and left him standing there with my sister. I felt at peace with myself, at the same time I left a part of me at the hospital, the part of me that needed a daddy's loving touch.

Kenny made arrangements for us to go on vacation the next day. We spent several days traveling slowly across the states. On the third day of our trip we arrived at our daughter Brandy's home in Indiana.

It was a warm spring day in 1993; we were celebrating Brandy's birthday. I received a phone call from my sister-in-law Kate. She informed me that Mom had died. I asked to speak to my dad. I was concerned about his well being and asked, "How are you doing, Dad?"

"I would be doing a hell of a lot better if it wasn't for you and your lies."

"I have to hang up now, Dad."

I immediately hung up the phone. I went into a yelling, screaming rage, pacing from one end of Brandy's little cottage to the other. When I became aware of the abusive language I was using in my daughter's home, I pulled on my shoes and headed for the door. "I'm sorry, everyone, but I just need to get away right now."

Kenny was swiftly behind me as I ran down the railroad tracks that were near the cottage. Still in rage, yelling coarse slurs, I just ran and ran until I was too exhausted to go any further. Kenny joined me as we continued down the tracks. By now, I was wailing and sobbing. Wailing for myself and sobbing over my loneliness. I had never felt this bleak in my entire life. Joy can be shared with others, but grieving is endured alone. Kenny hurt for me, but he couldn't understand my despair over the loss of my mom or the agonizing demarcation from my father.

Kenny and I returned to our home the night before Mom's funeral. I telephoned my sister-in-law Kate to find out the funeral details.

Dad had made the arrangements with Lynn to have my mother cremated. Dad decided to have the funeral service at my dad's church instead of at my mom's church. My dad was Baptist and my mom was of the Catholic faith.

I didn't sleep the night before the funeral. The next morning I called the funeral parlor that prepared Mom for the cremation. I wanted to see Mom one last time. The funeral director said, "I'm sorry, but they just took your mother's body to another city to be cremated."

"Please, sir, is there any way I can somehow catch up with the hearse carrying Mom? I need to say goodbye. She's my mom, you know."

"Mrs....,I know where the driver was going to stop for

gas. Do you want to hold on the line or I can call you back? I'll try to reach the driver before he gets too far."

"Thank you, I'll hold."

While waiting for the funeral director to make his calls to locate the driver of the hearse carrying my mom, I prayed.

"Hello, Mrs. ...I was able to reach the driver; he will bring the body of your mother back to the funeral parlor if you can make it here within the hour."

"Thank you, I'm leaving right now and will be there in forty-five minutes. Thanks a lot. You don't know how much this means to me."

When I got to the funeral parlor the director had my mom's body wrapped in a Ziplock bag, with Mom's head sticking out of the body bag. Brandy was with me in the room where Mom was laid.

The funeral director was apologetic, "I'm sorry, Mrs.... for you having to see your Mom like this. I was under the impression from your sister that everyone made their good-byes at the hospital. I really am sorry for not having her looking better."

"It's all right. I was out of town when Mom passed away. Thank you for doing this for my daughter and me."

"Mrs.... would you like me to say 'The Lord's Prayer' with you?"

"No, I can't say a prayer like that. No, I can't say 'Our Father,' because I can't forgive my dad or siblings for what they have done here. Mom never wanted to be cremated. Nor did she want a service in a strange church without even a showing of her body. No, I can't, I just can't say 'The Lord's Prayer'."

"I understand, Mrs.... I'll leave you alone. Take as much time as you need."

Brandy and I were alone with Mom's body. I took my make-up out of my purse and put it on Mom's face, cheeks, eyes, and lipstick for the final touch. I combed Mom's hair. Mom's hair was very shabby. I found a pair of sharp little scissors in my purse and trimmed her hair. "You look gorgeous now, Mom."

I rattled on and on. I'm not sure exactly what I said, but I do remember making her a promise. "I promise you Mom, I'll never be a victim again. I'll write our story, Mom, so that your life will account for something. You were a victim, Mom, right down to your funeral. I promise you I will fix it."

I kissed Mom, good-by, "I'll join you someday, Mom, in heaven."

I sat alone in the front pew of the church with my children and husband as the Baptist minister said the eulogy. My dad and siblings sat on the opposite side of the church. The last hymn was sung.

My dad turned to walk down the aisle to leave the church at the same time that I came to walk down the aisle. I reached out to Dad but he pushed me away; then he reached for my siblings. Without a word Dad walked away from me. I was hurt. I walked outside of the church and saw some of my friends standing by to console me.

The ladies at the Baptist church had a luncheon after the funeral service. I didn't want to stay. I felt ignored and snubbed by my birth family. Instead of staying at the church for lunch Kenny and I went to a nearby restaurant where our friends that were at the funeral service joined us. In the restaurant I was surrounded by my children and my friends who understood my pain.

I had noticed that Mom's Catholic friends were not at the funeral service held at the Baptist Church. I called Mom's priest and asked if he would have a service, or a Catholic Mass for Mom. The priest agreed and announced the Mass in the church bulletin for the upcoming week. I bought four large potted rose bushes that were in full bloom. After the Mass, I gave them to Mom's four closest friends to plant in their yards. I was surprised to see how many of Mom's Catholic friends showed up for the Mass. Mom's friends gave their condolences to me. I shared with them. Mom's friends thanked me over and over again for having the service so that they could make their goodbyes in her church.

I felt like Mom was a victim right down to her grave. When I had the Mass for Mom I felt that I gave a little something back to her. I could say goodbye to my mother because I did what I knew she would have wanted for her funeral, and that was to have her friends around in her church with her favorite flower, the red rose.

# Chapter Nine

# WHO WILL CARE FOR DAD?

Two weeks had passed after my mom's death, and I was feeling unquestionably lonely and abandoned. I decided to give my dad a chance at our relationship so I wrote him a letter.

Dear Daddy,

I continue to care about you, and love you with the deepest love a daughter could give to a dad. You asked me at the hospital when I confronted you why I didn't say anything sooner about you abusing me; I am enclosing a paper on flashbacks that hopefully will answer your questions.

I lost the closest person a child could ever have had, my mom. I hurt deeply and I feel a lot of pain, however, time will heal all. I haven't any regrets over the time or love that I shared with Mom and you. Everything that I gave to Mom and you was from my heart.

When my memories were restored to me, I had a

lot of anger to deal with. Throughout the time that I had been dealing with the anger, I still gave you my respect and love. I also taught my children to continue respecting you, for you will always be their grandfather.

I did not remove myself or my love from you and will continue to be there for you. However, I will respect you and allow you to have the space you need away from me. I pray in time that we can start over again, working on honesty and our friendship.

Love in Christ, your daughter, Sam

The day Dad got my letter, he phoned me. Dad was all choked up on the phone. "Hello, Sam, I received your letter today. It's lonely here without Mom and you. I really miss you Sam, can we get together soon?"

"I miss you, too, Dad; we need to try to make our situation better. However, I need to be honest about the whole ordeal that caused us to separate in the first place."

"I know you do…can we not talk about it now."

"All right, not today, but we need to talk soon."

"Bye, Sam, I love you."

"Bye, Dad."

Dad and I spoke every day over the phone the following week. He asked me to write thank you cards to those who sent cards of condolence. I agreed. I met Dad for the first time after the funeral at the funeral parlor where we picked out the cards that I would be sending. I agreed to go to Dad's home the next week to write the cards.

I had just gotten myself organized at my dad's kitchen table to type the thank you cards when Lynn and Louie arrived. Louie saw me there and decided to go back outdoors to have a cigarette. Lynn, however, talked to Dad for a couple of minutes and then headed straight for Mom's room. Lynn had no right being in Mom's bedroom, I thought, so I followed her. Looking back I know now that was Lynn's plot to set me up for an argument. Lynn's plot worked; she goaded me into an argument. I was getting angrier by the second.

I pulled my fist back; I wanted to wallop a hard blow to Lynn's arrogant face. Lynn was within inches of my face screaming sarcastic slurs into my ear. Lynn must have thought that she was winning because I showed traits of anger. For a brief moment I was reliving my childhood and the need to survive. I was reclaiming the knowledge of knowing how to fight to make it in the household of my birth family, but something stopped me; I was brought back to now, to the fact that I wasn't any longer a child but an adult with adult survival skills. My hand still in a fist, I slowly lowered my arm to my side. Lynn probed and needled me with sarcasm, making sure to point out my anger. "You're damn right, I'm angry," I said. "At least I can admit it!"

I knew that my anger was only an emotion that couldn't hurt me as long as I took ownership of it and claimed it as my own. I decided not to give way to the negative side of the anger that I felt.

My fist relaxed, I turned and walked out of Mom's bedroom and into the kitchen, where Lynn followed me. Lynn continued to hurl accusations against my person as she had done several times before. With each encounter, the severity of Lynn's name calling and harassing behavior had become more straining on my emotional well being. Knowing that an angry violent person, like my sister, gets her highs from trying to set other people into a tailspin, I decided I wasn't going to dance her dance or play her game of dysfunctional behavior. Neither was I going to give Lynn the satisfaction to gloat by getting me to argue with her. However, this time I wasn't going to sit by idly and allow Lynn to hurl critical derogatory statements against me as a person. I was working a master plan in my mind to over-throw Lynn's brutality against my person without her spinning a web of deception to suck the life from me.

I booted up my laptop computer and sat down at my dad's kitchen table. I began to process thank you cards in response to the many sympathy cards that we had received on behalf of mom's death. My dad sat to the left of me. Lynn came from the bedroom and sat to my right. Lynn was still trying to get me to react; I tuned her out.

I had learned to read Lynn's every move, and I knew when her foot starts to shake, she is about to attack me with some sort of brutal wordpower game. When Lynn doesn't seem to get the response she wants from her victim, she usually rises and paces. When Lynn paces, I learned that the big hit below the belt with her words is on its way. Sure enough, Lynn got up from the table and started to pace the floor.

When Lynn started to pace, I became very aware of my breathing and was using some relaxation skills I had learned; I took full knowledge of my body cues and was aware of my inner being. I reached out to God in prayer, asking for His wisdom and deliverance. I had my whole emotional self in control. I took slow, long, soothing breaths which gave me stamina. I was feeling powerful, collected, and in full control.

I watched Lynn pace; I sensed her losing all aspects of control of her emotions; the heat of her anger was rising. I thought about what I was going to accomplish through Lynn's anger. I decided that this would be a good time to face the truth with her. My thinking was clear and alert. I was going to manage this conversation despite whatever Lynn tried to use as her weapon of attack on my character. I knew that I would have to block out Lynn's abusive words and stick to the issues that I had planned for this showdown scheduled by God.

Lynn tried to arouse my anger. She used the same tactics that she had used earlier when we were in the bedroom. Lynn was aware that she wasn't making any progress with her strategy. Lynn shifted maneuvers, and she brought up what had happened at the hospital between Dad and me when I confronted him at the elevator doors.

At the hospital when I was getting unto the elevator, I saw Lynn lurching beside the wall in the corridor. When Lynn huddled against the wall, I realized that the nosy wretch was listening around the corner of the corridor to the private conversation Dad and I were having.

A month had passed since that day at the hospital. It must have been a disappointing surprise for Lynn when she arrived at Dad's house and found me there. Lynn didn't know about Dad's confession to me, nor that Dad said he didn't mean to hurt his girls, plural. Neither did Lynn know that Dad had called me to work on resolving the pain which occurred in Dad's and my relationship thirty-five years ago.

In my mind I recalled a quick synopsis of how Lynn had hurt my mom with her letter eleven years ago when she claimed that my parents had abused her. My memory recalled how Lynn isolated herself from my parent's presence for ten years. I recalled how Mom tried to make contact with Lynn and how she would curse Mom each time.

I remembered how Mom hurt over the absence of her oldest daughter. This absence caused mom to be depressed, full of anxiety, and physical ailments which were linked to the anger within Mom. I recalled how Lynn and Mom made peace with one another but how Lynn still victimized her when Mom was living with me. Lynn refused to call Mom at my house because Lynn's vengeance was turned on me. I remembered the ten months that Mom struggled for her life between heart attacks and then Mom gave up and died. The death certificate showed that Mom died from heart failure. However, the death certificate didn't tell the whole story about how Mom's heart was broken by Lynn.

I was always there for Mom, yet as Mom experienced her first heart attack in my home in 1992, Mom's first outcry was for Lynn as we left for the hospital. I felt hurt because Mom was still trying to get Lynn's acceptance and didn't realize the agony I had been through because of Lynn.

You bet I was angry at Lynn's attacks vented toward Mom all those years. I had skills to handle the attacks, but Mom was like a sheep ready for the slaughter. Mom was weak and full of shame and false guilt that Lynn and others laid on her.

I was still in control showing little if any emotion after the quick trip my mind took reminiscing the past like a tape on fast forward. Lynn had her focus on part of the story, the part of her eavesdropping in the hospital corridor. Lynn brought up the accusations that I had made against Dad on that day at the hospital.

I commented, "It's none of your business what went on between Dad and me."

"It's my business when it involves Dad," Lynn stated sarcastically.

I felt bad for my dad but I couldn't let it go. Lynn gave me a perfect setup. I looked straight at Lynn, standing close to my dad and I said, "What, Lynn are you going to take Mom's place to protect and shield Dad from having to take responsibility for his actions? Are you going to go to your grave like Mom without a life of your own because you're to busy covering up the abuse? By the way Lynn, what did you mean in your letter to Mom when you said, 'they abused you'?"

Lynn replied, "I don't know what you're talking about."

"Lynn I still have the letters, Mom gave them to me for safekeeping."

Lynn looked to Dad for protection. However, instead of giving Lynn the support that she was looking for, Dad hung his head in his folded hands and said nothing.

Lynn's husband Louie walked through the kitchen door. In a rage of anger Lynn turned to Louie to bail her out. Lynn knew that she had lost ground with me. Lynn told Louie about my accusations against her about the theft of different objects from our parent's property, which both Mom and Dad witnessed. Lynn related to Louie how I accused her of abusing Mom. Lynn also told her version of my words concerning the abuse that Lynn was so compelled to cover up and deny. I found Lynn's story slightly amusing, for Lynn must have been listening to me as she was pretty accurate in relating the story back to Louie the way that I had intended it to be.

While Lynn was filling Louie in on the happenings before his arrival, it gave me time to pray, to catch my breath, and to get my focus and insight on managing my maneuvers with the next culprit, Louie. Louie sat down in the empty chair to my right. Dad, still sitting to the left of me, raised his head and Dad became a bystander for what was about to take place. Lynn stood opposite of me at the end of the table pacing back and forth throwing around her only weapon, name calling. I tuned Lynn's words out and focused on Louie's sweating brow. That gave me a clue that Louie, like Lynn was also out of control with his emotions. I wondered if the piercing words of my letter that I had delivered to Louie at the hospital accusing him of being a child molester were running through Louie's mind.

Louie thought that he would be coy with me and said, "Why are you telling all these lies?"

Perfect, Louie was playing right into my ploy of managing the conversation. I looked right over his head. I am sure Louie thought I was looking at him, and I said, "That is exactly what I would expect to hear from a perpetrator."

Louie shot questions of accusation against me while

trying to turn the truth around to make me look like the villain. I found Louie's accusations amusing and ironic for he set himself up by portraying the four stages of an abuser making me realize what a perpetrator he really was. Louie set the stage giving me perfect opportunity to disclose his victimization of other women in my community, one was my friend Julie. Lynn didn't seem surprised to hear such truth; however, she tried to deny the reality of the truth by discrediting me by calling my husband some vulgar names. Lynn was on a witch hunt with name-calling. However, I was on a roll and nothing could pierce the protective shell that God had surrounded me with.

One of Lynn's accusations caught my ear. Lynn in rage asked me, "How many boys did you abuse?"

A quick glimpse of years earlier when Louie begged us to take his oldest son before Lynn destroyed him made me wonder if my fears were validated of her being a child abuser.

Lynn's words to me about abusing boys and details of which she stated in abuse of boys gave her away; I believed she abused at least one of her sons and maybe more. I wondered if Lynn might have abused any of the boys that she babysat for. However, I stored that information in the back of my mind to reflect on at a later date.

Louie was losing the verbal battle with me and he knew it. Louie's voice started to crack and shake; his lips were thin showing his anger. Louie's brow was sweating profusely, along with his hands shaking. Louie lost all control in the process to stop the truth from my lips. In desperation to get the control from me, Louie threatened to take my life.

Once again I was unmoved by Louie's threat, and I commented, "Is that a threat, Louie?"

Louie said, "I'll get someone to get rid of you, wipe you out."

"Notice, Louie, I'm really afraid." I commented with

confidence, "That's the kind of threats I would expect from a perpetrator."

Neither Louie nor Lynn could break through the barrier that God had placed around me. Lynn and Louie left defeated; I stood strong with praise and thanksgiving upon my lips to my God for the confidence, strength, and victory that was mine as I took my life back.

I felt a slight bit of pity for my dad, an old man of eighty-four. Dad was reaping the effects of child abuse that had gone on for several generations.

Three years have passed sense my mom's passing away. Dad and I have had time to restructure and heal our relationship. Dad is learning to be open and a little more honest with me about our past.

In August of 1995 Dad trusted me enough to share the memories he had carried from his past. Dad's memories consisted of him being sexually abused by his stepmother in Dad's early adolescence years. It took Dad almost seventy years to share hidden secrets of childhood sexual abuse.

I'm not excusing Dad's behavior toward me, but I now understand Dad better. In sexual abuse cases I learned that the victim of abuse will continue being a victim of others abusing them; the abused will become abusers themselves, or the abused will become caretakers. I guess I am a caretaker; I will always take care of Dad.

# PART 2

## Healing of the Soul

### Where Compassion and Love Triumph

# Chapter Ten

# DAD'S CONTINUED CARE

Over the next seven years, Dad spent most of his weekends with us. I started to notice his bodily cleanliness was decreasing as the weeks went by. The director of the senior citizen center also called to inform me of his bodily stench and to say something needed to be done about it as his colleagues were complaining when he sat by them for dinner. Brandy was home for a summer visit so we went on a rendezvous to Dad's house in the small village where Dad resided. We picked up seven garbage bags of clothes that were sprawled throughout his bedroom and kitchen. It was obvious the clothes were worn continually without washing. In sorting the clothes at the laundry mat, our nostrils were filled with the smell of ammonia from the dried urine stains.

I put Dad's clean, poorly maintained wardrobe back in his closet and drawers. In addition I bought a new clothes hamper and told him when the basket got full to bring it to me, and I would wash them. I also took several changes of clothes to my house and put them in the room where he slept when he visited us. When I would ask about his laundry, he would comment that he was able to wash them himself.

It wasn't long before we noticed Dad's health slipping. He began to forget information or medication, repeated the same stories several times over, and sometimes would not be sure of what day of the week or year it was. Still, it wasn't long before the stench of urine would infiltrate his garments. I would then make sure Dad would shower and wash his clothes before returning to his own residence. That's when I talked him into making his weekend stays a little longer. From then on he would come to my home on Wednesdays after he delivered senior citizen meals and would stay until Monday when I would leave for work. Dad felt needed and functional as he oversaw our teenage sons get off to school and sometimes gave them a ride to and from school events. Many times he would meet me at the door with a smirk on his face and I would know that he did something that he thought would please me, like peeling potatoes or brushing the dogs. I always made a big point at the dinner table about how appreciative I was that Grandpa did such and such for us. We noticed a big change in him from the day he arrived until the day he left. We concluded that when he was home, he wasn't taking his medication or eating properly.

Unfortunately we received another phone call from the director of the senior citizens center with complaints of his poor hygiene and forgetfulness in delivering meals to shut-in people. Many times he would forget where to go with the meals, so they had to finally ask him to give up the deliveries.

Dad prided himself that he had a job delivering meals at the ripe old age of ninety. I never let on that I knew he was asked to give up his meal delivery job; he never mentioned it to me either.

Brandy was home for Thanksgiving so we surprised grandpa with a visit. It was four months since her previous visit, and when we arrived, the place was in shambles. In the living room was a gray enamel scrub bucket placed next to his lounging chair. In the bucket were old pasty crusts, chicken bones and the likes. Cracker crumbs, empty cookie packages, along with candy wrappers, old mildew rolls, and bread were stacked up along side of his chair and end table.

I was embarrassed for Brandy. She dug right in and started to clean up the ruin; however, when she moved grandpa's chair to vacuum under it there was a nest of bugs and worms living off the decomposing rations. This was upsetting enough for any person, but even more so to my pregnant daughter. I took over the vacuuming while she sorted through stacks upon stacks of mail sprawled throughout the living room, kitchen, bedroom, and staircase landing.

On the kitchen cupboard was a convoy of mouse traps encircling a variation of frosted donuts. In asking Dad why the mouse traps were bordered around the donuts, his reply was, "Look at the mouse shit on them!" He assumed the chocolate sprinkles on the donuts were mice dung. Humor was needed to offset my awareness that Dad could no longer care for himself.

I informed my brother of Dad's situation. Ben lived only one mile from Dad on a forty of land Dad had given to him. Ben drove semi-truck over the road and was gone for days on end, but said his wife would check in on Dad occasionally.

By December the situation became hopeless. Kenny and I talked Dad into coming to live with us on a temporary basis for the winter. The moving date was over the Christmas holidays, and my brother was informed of the transition. Lynn never kept much contact with Dad, but when Ben gave her the news of Dad's move, she called to tell Dad that Louie was coming to get him. Dad later told me that he left the house and hid out on an old gravel road outside the village of his residence, until he was sure Louie would be gone. He was afraid Louie would force him to go with him. There were some deep-rooted truck tire tracks where someone peeled out of the driveway which Dad assumed were Louie's. Later that week Dad told me that Lynn came over and demanded things from the house and he finally said, "Take the damn things!" She did and that was the last he heard from her. Kate also helped herself to things she wanted. One would think he had died the way the vultures came in to peck away at the ruins of an old man's dwelling place.

There were times that I did not feel at ease with Dad in my home, especially when he would come to my bedroom door to say goodnight. I just didn't want him in my room; this was my place of sanctuary. In the back of my mind I realized I had unfinished emotional business to take care of. I just didn't want to go that route again! Why can't it just be over; why can't I just let it go? However, I knew it was God working on the inner me to bring about more healing to my relationship with Dad.

## Chapter Eleven

# BEHIND THE PADLOCKED DOOR

I couldn't shake it any longer. This was the second summer that I felt the discomfort and unease within my soul. Fear gripped my heart each time the thought of going back where the abortion took place exhausted my inner peace. I tried hard to push the memories back into the chasm of my subconscious. However, the effort to resolve the impending inner drive to go to Minnesota pursued my mind and haunted my soul with fear and anguish. I had to go back and face the fixation that I could no longer restrain. Realistically, I had to follow the strong urge or continue to chastise myself for something that I had no control over; however, stage management was mine to control this time around. So I thought. The contemplation of God working to familiarize me with the degeneracy of immorality and injustice done to me in the doctor's office thirty plus years earlier somehow gave me a drive to continue the route God was sending me on. My fear and anger seemed to settle somewhat as I put my trust in my God to lead the way back. I talked to Kenny about the need to visit the town and setting of where my baby was taken from me.

Kenny knew my journeys thus far, for he was my strength through my emotional upheavals of memory flashbacks. At times even God seemed to abandon me on a galaxy void of authenticity. The only rational part of my life was Kenny. Kenny's compassionate eyes calculated mine as I shared with him the impetuous trip that I was in dire need to make. After listening meticulously, Kenny initiated turning the trip into a vacation and taking time for us. We made arrangements for Lee and Ken to watch over Grandpa while we were gone. Ben also agreed to have Dad stay with him for a weekend.

A few weeks later we were sightseeing in the vastness of the wilderness outside the remote town I once lived in. I recalled happy times at the park and along the beach. We laughed as I told him of the things I did with my friends. Speaking of friends, I wanted to go to my best friend's house. Unbelievable, but I remembered the address on Washington Street and the exact location.

I didn't recognize the elderly man at the door. Stepping into the doorway brought back memories and the recollections of shenanigans Jane and I pulled just to spend the night at either her house or mine, mostly hers. We practically spent that whole summer together. After a quick explanation of who I was and who I was looking for, I found out that Jane's mother was in a nearby nursing home.

I couldn't distinguish Mrs. Lewis from the other residents and had to have her pointed out to me. I sat and talked with her about Jane. She complained and went on about her aches and pains and how hard it was to persevere. She seemed weary and exhausted just from existing. It seemed our tête-à-tête was ended as I made my goodbyes. She became alert, her weary eyes gazed into mine as she pleaded, "Oh, please don't tell Jane about me and my situation and how bad I feel because I don't want her to worry about me. Please tell her that I'm fine." I promised her that I would relate her message to her daughter.

I wondered, how a woman confined to a place with hopelessness all around her, could pull from within the absolute caring of her offspring and not of her woes? I bent over and kissed her on the forehead, and my eyes filled with tears; memories of pleasurable and joyous times overcame my whole continence. Like eating ice cream too fast and developing a brain freeze; I felt the thaw of frozen memories as the renewing of the love and approval I felt in this woman's home once again touch my heart.

Kenny's burly hand reached for mine as we walked down the corridors out of the nursing home building to the car. I reached for the car door handle as Kenny reached for me. He put his arm around me and held me close. I needed that assurance. I felt a resurrection of lost feelings continue to fill my inner being with softness. A softness in me that was lost because of untruth that penetrated my soul to control me. As a preteen I was too afraid to acknowledge that the Lewis family could really love someone like me. 'Someone Like Me'. I had to chuckle at that thought. I knew about that learned behavior in which I overlooked all feelings. Even the good ones seemed to be misconstrued because of inappropriate treatment to my mental and physical well being. I felt God was now showing me appropriate feelings for the proper occasion.

We went to a wild life expo. We really enjoyed the adventure and the time to relax. Afterwards we picked up some brochures and headed for our motel to plan our outings for the following day. In the morning Kenny went to get some coffee and came back with apples, blueberry muffins, and raspberry yogurt. We lay across the bed, spread out our brochures, ate and talked over our plans. We packed up and headed for our next adventure. We were driving in circles so Kenny decided to stop and ask for directions. Why do we even make plans because they seem so futile when God has his own agenda? When Kenny finished getting directions, I felt a nudge inside to ask where the clinic was located. We got in the car; Kenny looked at me and we both knew where we needed to be.

I wasn't sure what I was going to do as we headed for the clinic. Would I go in and confront the abortionist? Would I be irrational and make a scene? Within I knew that would be incongruous to who I am now. Being acquainted with who I am, I understood me; I would restrain myself and show complete control. So what am I going to do? I had no plan but God did. We found the clinic. Kenny pulled up in the parking lot and sat quietly as I positioned myself closer to him in the car; saying nothing, feeling nothing, no hatred, no animosity just a sadness and feeling of effortlessness hung over me. "It's time to go," I said.

Kenny started the car. God's constant companionship had led me throughout the city the past couple of days, yet my traveling along God's path was still not completed. I still didn't know why God dragged me through the memories of this town, or his reasoning for me to sit quietly outside the clinic in the parking lot.

I felt a strong sense to continue my journey along the school fence where I envisioned the frail forlorn little girl walking the fence line feeling lost and alone. My dad's company relocated him in this new town. I was too shy to reach out to anyone in this neighborhood, so the whole summer I stayed by myself secluded in the attic of our apartment building. An electrical surge of feeling went through me, an imperious need to go to the apartment where I shared this loneliness with a box of color crayons and oil paintings by number.

We rode around a couple of blocks. I wasn't sure of the address. That struck me kind of funny; I could remember Jane's full address and had no recollection of my own. I even recalled her phone number and had no clue what mine was. Stop, I remember the porch and long twisted steps coming down from the apartment next to ours. "Go around again. That's the house!" It never had a fence around it before and the bushes were replaced with playground equipment. I walked up to the door, hesitated, and was about to walk away when that surge overcame me once again. I knocked and a rather stout young woman opened the door. She knew of me as I had spoken to her on the phone the day before when I was looking for her sister-in-law, Barbie. I told her that I once lived there and was curious about the place. She invited me in.

There were toys from one end of the house to the other. Not just toys but actual gymnastic equipment for tots was placed in one of the rooms along with sleeping mats. All play areas could be seen from the middle of the apartment. I was invited to sit on a rather low worn orange and brown tweed couch with a horse blanket cover. In a large open space opposite from where I sat was an arrangement of colossal vehicles; a fire engine, army jeep, and a car the kids could drive around by using their feet, a rocking horse and a flying airplane on two spring posts. Behind the vehicles were shelves reaching from the floor to the ceiling. The shelves were filled with more toys, books and papers along with cutting tools, coloring, painting, and craft items to be used in this day care setting. The shelves that little hands could reach were empty except for finger prints on the dusty shelves. I was inconspicuous to the three children in the dining area. They were absorbed in the movie *Beauty and the Beast* while eating a snack of goldfish crackers and cheese spread with apple juice in sippy cups. Behind the snack area was a double door which opened to the kitchen. There were little plates with kittens and puppies in the drain board along with plastic cartoon character glasses. Cupboard door hinges were broken, revealing the contents of boxed pudding, Jell-O, macaroni and cheese, hamburger helper, along with all sorts of crackers, treats, and dried fruit. On the counter top sat a basket of brown bananas and a half eaten apple next to several handmade vases from juice bottles, all dripping with Elmer's Glue.

Stressed out from the Early Childhood politics, Peggy the young woman I had just met, decided to quit her job and open a daycare. Peggy had married George, whose parents were our landlords, and together were the owners of the house since his parents had died. Peggy and I had so much in common; we both have degrees in early childhood education and have had a daycare at one time. We shared ideas and goals that we both have concerning children. I couldn't believe the friendship that developed instantly as we talked. The children's movie was just about over and Peggy was expecting more children in a little while, so our time together was ending.

Finally, I got around to asking Peggy if I could see the attic where I had spent most of my time while living in this house. She had leased the attic to a man who used it for storage and unfortunately she didn't have a key. She did, however, lead me through the kitchen, which led us into the entry way of the attic and the apartment I once lived in.

The door to my old apartment was closed. Opposite that apartment entrance was a doorway leading to the attic. I fixed my gaze upon the staircase and slowly moved my eyes upward toward the top. There I saw the door to the attic entrance, padlocked shut. There in the attic, locked up forever, were my color crayons and memories etched in the mind of a naive child who lost her ability to feel.

One of the kids in the daycare called to Miss Peggy and she excused herself for a minute. I stood motionless; I was caught in time, a silhouette of that little girl in the attic innocently coloring behind the locked door. In my mind I unlocked the door and knelt down beside her, running my hand along her long blonde, dirty limp hair. "Everything is ok," I whispered, "for the truth is in you. Your memories are all you have; you can trust them for they are you, and you can feel without being afraid."

I started for the daycare kitchen. Turning, I took one last look with my eyes up the stairwell to the attic and across to the closed door of my old apartment and walked away. I swallowed hard and went back into the daycare setting.

Other children arrived and laughter filled the room as they joined in playtime with their friends. Behind the walls of this happy setting was the bathroom where my baby was aborted and flushed; while my mother listened as I cried in agony. I felt this was a consolation for my baby Breann, like a memorial to her; a daycare in honor of her filled with children and cared for by the loving nurturing caregiver, Miss Peggy.

I slowly walked half a block to the car, where Kenny had waited patiently for me for over an hour. I got in; he didn't start the car and didn't say anything. He just sat there with his arm limply around my shoulder. Slowly pulling his arm away, he left me to my feelings. Gentle tears flowed down my checks. I didn't understand it; I never had experienced such a tranquil cry before. I felt like a warm summer brook was flowing through me and down my face. I have had tears of anger and despair; I have shed tears of sorrow, tears of joy, but never before had I experienced tears of peace. The tears were healing the memories locked up inside me. God made peace with my past by bringing me to a padlocked door beyond the daycare. He renewed my feelings and reminded me of friendship and people who really loved me for who I was. It was an enjoyable quest mapped out by God.

Dad was anxious to see us when we got home. He related how much he missed us and how he hated the smoke filled house of Ben's. Dad followed me around like a puppy dog for the next few days.

I was scrapping old wrought iron lawn furniture in the

garage when Dad joined in to help. Several pieces later and much conversation passed when I asked Dad if he enjoyed the work. He "loathed" the work was his response.

"So why do it?" I asked.

"To be with you; I enjoy our talks."

I almost cried, but I came back with, "I detest this work also but it has to be done."

Dad chuckled, put out his hand in a hand shake, and said, "Put it here. We are so much alike."

The rest of the summer was filled with positive memories from my adult life that we shared. Building our house, fishing stories with my children, Kenny and Dad's hunting experiences and the many times Mom would get upset with us because we were like two peas in a pod were all fond memories.

I was sitting up in bed reading when I heard a light knock on my bedroom door. I looked up and smiled. It was Dad, "Just come to say goodnight." I got up from the bed and went over and gave him a hug. He whispered, "Goodnight, Sam, I love you."

"Goodnight, Dad," I squeezed him tight, "Don't let the bedbugs bite, and I love you, too." This was the beginning of a bona fide, trusting father-daughter relationship, which God intended it to be from the start.

# Chapter Twelve

# FRIENDSHIPS NEVER DIE

Vera and Ike were elderly people that retired and moved back to our community from the city. We attended the same functions and church activities. Ike remembered what a scallywag Kenny was in his youth and took a liking to him. The couple became our espousal parents as well as our mentors in our young Christian walk. Vera was my spiritual mom. Kenny and Ike were a lot a like, full of pranks and teasing. Of course, Vera and I were the focus.

In an emotional stupor when the flashbacks started to invade my mind, I went like a child to Vera and Ike and blurted out what happened to me as a child. I sobbed, they sobbed, and Ike held me like his own child trying to sooth over my pain. Over the next couple of years our hearts grew together in tenderness caring for each others well-being, my emotional and their physical.

Vera had her second stroke and didn't survive it. I helped Ike with the funeral arrangements. Ike became totally dependent on us.

I went to visit Brandy for several days. Ike knew when I was getting back and called me as soon as I walked in the door. His dog had died and he wouldn't let anyone take care of it until I got home. I offered to go get the dog and burry it by our cabin. It was a humid summer day; little did I know that the dog had died three days prior. We got the dog into a large galvanized garbage can, with its head sticking out the top of the can. I headed for the cabin, calling Kenny from the cell phone to meet me at the cabin. Kenny arrived as I was digging the hole. He finished digging, and as we tipped the can over to dump the reeking animal into its grave, the animal burst open leaving yellow excretions down my arm. I sprinted to the woods where I dry heaved while Kenny finished the task at hand, laughing hysterically at my dilemma. What one must do for a friend! This is just one of the many memories my family and I chuckle over when we gather.

Ike had heart complications and was hospitalized for several days. He called to tell me that they were going to release him that day; I asked what time I was to come and get him. He was quiet for a little while and then said, "They're going to put me in a nursing home." Without hesitation, I responded, "You're coming to live with us." After much discussion and tears, he thanked me and the plans were put into action.

Dad was standing by and wanted to know how Ike was doing. I told Dad about them wanting to put Ike in a nursing home, and his response, like mine was, "He can't go to a home; he has to come here."

Whoops! I forgot to include Kenny; but all was well when Kenny said there was no alternative, for he was part of the family. The arrangements were made to get Ike home with us.

Dad was in his bedroom packing up his things that were on his dresser. I noticed some of his clothes were on his bed with his suitcase next to them. "What are you doing Dad?" With a serious tone in his voice Dad responded, "Ike can't climb the stairs so I'll take the room downstairs. Ike can have my room."

"Dad, you're ninety-one-years-old. You can't go downstairs; Ike can share the room with our youngest son."

In my household, were two old men, one of them legally blind and the other one hard of hearing. What a circus we had going, but what a joy! Ike was never a burden. I thought I took Ike in to be a help to a weary old friend, but as it turned out, God gave him to us as a blessing. Ike knew me like a father, and he would find spare moments to take time alone with me just to give substantial support that a father might give to a daughter. I shared with Ike many of my frustrations. He always seemed to know how to encourage me or when to crack a joke when I was too solemn.

The two elderly men became great buddies, depending on one another. Dad could still drive, and Ike would give him directions so they could go do elderly things. Two obstinate old men, at times, if Dad wouldn't heed what Ike was saying Ike would say, "Sam said," as if what Sam said was law.

In October of 2000 I was called out of my classroom at work by Kenny telling me that Ike had suffered a massive heart-attack at home. What a loss to all of us, especially Dad.

The November deer season had just opened. Dad was rushing to get his truck cleared of snow so he could meet Kenny at camp. Dad came back into the house for his gloves when I heard a thud and a groan from his bedroom. His face seemed distorted, and his speech was slurred. Somehow I managed to pick him up and lay him on his bed. His pulse and breathing seemed normal. He muttered that he wasn't in any pain. I thought he might have fallen. I left him alone while I went to get Kenny, who was a couple miles away from the house. Dad's face and speech were back to normal when we got back home, but we took him to the clinic nearby for a check-up just the same. Dr. Jacobs called it TIA (transient ischemic attack). TIAs are a warning sign of an impending stroke, however they usually resolve within a few minutes to an hour.

On Christmas Day, 2000, we had just finished eating; I was getting everyone dessert when Kenny hollered, "Grandpa, Grandpa!" Dad's head went to his plate and he once again was having symptoms of a TIA. The ambulance arrived and Dad showed no signs of recovery. We raced to the hospital praying all the way. We got there ahead of the ambulance; anticipating the worst. When the door to the ambulance was open, there sat Dad wanting to do a polka with the attendant. They kept him a couple of days to observe him. The doctors put a pacemaker in as a preventive measure against a heart-attack or stroke.

Dad decided for himself not to drive any longer because of fear of having a TIA on the road. He drove his old rusty red S10 Chevy over to our son's home a block away and signed the title over to his great-grandson, Ken III, age five, and walked home.

Dad was now homebound. Kenny and I had to work, so Dad was home alone during the week. We noticed him quickly digress in his health. He was depressed; he missed his old chum Ike, and now he couldn't get out during the week to visit and chew the fat with other senior citizens in our area.

Dad went downhill quickly. I had to clean up after him as he started to defecate in his underwear. I gave him Depends but that humiliated him, and it wasn't long before he started to hide them and his underwear in his room.

Dr. Jacobs suggested we look into convalescent homes, as it might take up to a year to get him into one. I checked every facility, got the paper work, and on the way out the door, ripped the application up as I couldn't tolerate what I saw. Dad would be just as unhappy if not more in places like the ones I checked out.

I ran into an old friend who shared her experience with me about her dad being in a nursing home thirty miles from where we lived. She highly recommended the facility.

Kenny and I went several times to visit my friend's dad, mostly to check the place out. It had a real homey atmosphere. The staff was like family and treated each other with respect, showing a real love for their job and a love for the residents. This showed by their words of affirmation and the tenderhearted nurturing they gave to the people under their care. I noticed that there wasn't an odor like many of the nursing homes I visited. I believed that this facility was an answer to prayer.

In April I filled out an application for Dad at the Woodland Convalescent Nursing Home. I was told that there was a long waiting list. That was all right with me as school was out in a couple of months and I would be home for the summer to care for Dad and to get him out of the house whenever needed.

Three days after dropping off dad's application at Woodland Convalescent Nursing Home, I received a phone call from the director of the facility. They wanted to meet with us about my father's care. My friend's father had passed away, and we were highly recommended by my friend's family.

Within a week Dad had a new home. He was apprehensive, but I promised if he didn't like living at Woodland that he could come back home when school got out in June and I would be home for him. We shook hands in agreement.

## Chapter Thirteen

# BONDS THAT CAN'T BE BROKEN

Dad adjusted favorably to his new living quarters at Woodland Convalescent Home. Several widowed ladies had their eye on him as a new prospect and he loved the attention. He would sing to them, "Show me the way to go home. I'm tired and I want to go to bed. I had a couple of drinks about an hour ago and they went right to my head..." At first I was embarrassed, and commented to the staff, "You're going to think he's a lush, but actually he doesn't even drink." I thought to myself, "Why can't he sing "Jesus Loves Me"?"

It wasn't long before he got to know everyone. Marshal was his roommate, and they hit it off from the start. Dad found his companion; they walked everywhere together, dining hall, activities such as bingo, sing-a-longs, crafts, bowling, and outside pleasures to name a few.

Wherever Dad went in life, he seemed to always make himself useful and available. Before long he knew all the wheelchair residents. He would wheel them to wherever there was something going on, so they didn't miss any of the events.

I got to know everyone by name and over the next eighteen months built ties with all of them. I got over my embarrassment when Dad sang his songs. Everyone, including the nursing staff, loved Dad and commented on how he perked everyone up and keeps their momentum going. When I brought Dad home on holidays or for the weekend, he was anxious to get back, afraid he might miss something.

A picnic was planned with all the families of residents and before long Dad and I were a part of the residents' extended families. Dad and I danced the polka to live music at the picnic-not bad for ninety-two.

I loved the staff and everyone associated with the nursing home. I would volunteer my help whenever possible. I work with mentally challenged kids and would take the students over to socialize with the residents and also to help out where they could. The students and the residents looked forward to seeing each other. On Fridays, Dad went swimming with the students at the community pool. One of the students felt helpful and privileged to help his newly acquainted grandpa find the locker room each week.

The staff commented several times about the loving relationship and fondness Dad and I had for each other. Dad carried a school picture of me in his wallet; he would embarrass me by showing it to everyone and telling them time and time again that I was his baby daughter.

Susan, the director, reinforced the love my dad shared with me and how I cared for him. Deep inside, the longing I once had for a father's love was complete. Dad fulfilled his fatherly role to his baby girl.

## Chapter Fourteen

# THE BEGINNING OF
# THE END

W e were sitting in the middle of the Sunday worship service when a phone call came for Kenny. Earlier in the morning we found out that my grandson was running a high fever; therefore, I thought the call was one concerning him. Kenny came back to the pew with the phone message and said that it was my daughter-in-law, but it had nothing to do with her son; she was informing us of a phone call she had just received from one of my nephews. Ben was dead, "Ben, Ben who? Was it my nephew or my brother?" Kenny said it was my brother.

"But they call his son, Benny, are you sure it wasn't him?"

Kenny said, "No, it is your brother, Sam!"

I felt the coldness of the January air solidify like an iceberg, as it penetrated through my spine. I sat in the church pew numb, perplexed about the unfounded interruption. I felt unresponsive to the hearsay. Time seemed to stop; everything around me was on hold like a long pause on a rented movie. Abruptly the interlude was over. Someone seemed to have clicked the remote, and it seemed like the movie was going on fast forward as Kenny's words penetrated my soul. "My brother's dead. Can't be! Can it?" I looked up at Kenny, our eyes caught; I could see consternation on his face like so many other times as my life unfolded; another horrendous pursuit to add to the pathway of my life.

Kenny escorted me out of the church where I phoned my brother's home only to hear the news, "Ben died this morning. He had one pain in his chest and within a half hour he was dead."

How could it be? He was only sixty-four years old. When I'm not ready to shoulder the daunting circumstances before me, it's my ritual to enter a state of mind in which I block out realism, especially when the state of affairs is out of my control. Okay, my brother died today, but I have plans to go to Green Bay with another couple. Insensitive to the goings-on around me I went the two-hundred mile round trip just to go out for dinner with our friends. "Wouldn't you like to spend time with your family?" LoAnn asked.

"No, not really..., my sister Lynn will be there. She needs to be there more than I. Ben was all she had left of the family."

In checking with my dad's doctor, he didn't think it wise for my dad to go to the funeral; at age ninety-three it would be too much of a shock to his system to see his only son lying in the casket. Approximately twenty years earlier I took my dad to his younger brother's funeral and watched him whimper over the dead body saying repetitively, "According to Hoyle it should be me there. I'm the oldest!" I don't think I could handle watching Dad go through that again, nor did I want to. The death of his son would be just too much of a hardship for him to absorb.

We were told that Dad's old pastor was doing the service for my brother, the same pastor who delivered my mom's eulogy. The pastor had gone to the nursing home and told my dad of my brother's death. The pastor was pretty persistent that Dad should be at the funeral ceremony. I thought it best to take the doctor's recommendation and not put my dad through such an ordeal.

Kenny and I went to see Dad just before we went to the funeral. Dad did not once speak of Ben's death, so we didn't bring it up. He either didn't remember the pastor telling him, or he blocked it out. We all deal with death differently, and I allowed Dad to deal with Ben's death in his own way, in his own time.

I stood before Ben's casket; I felt a sense of peace, knowing my brother trusted in Jesus as his Savior after the Viet Nam War. I whispered to him, "I'll see you in heaven someday." In the same breath I said, "You can't hurt anyone ever again". What did I mean? Oh, I knew exactly what I meant as I could feel and hear the turmoil in his daughter's unremitting weeping in the background, knowing that she too was a victim of my brother's abuse.

In talking with my niece the day prior to the funeral, she stated that she had forgiven her dad, but yet she had so many emotions drowning her that she didn't know what to think. "You feel as if fireworks are going off inside of you," I said. Through swollen, tear filled eyes, my niece looked at me; our eyes locked as she fixed her gaze upon me as if to say; "Someone knows exactly what I'm talking about." Inside her feelings were validated; we instantly bonded. How did I know? I've been there!

Weeks had passed since my brother's funeral. Disheartened by the memory of some rather large man, whom Dad stated he had never seen before, told him "Ben hung himself and they buried him right there." Where he got 'hung himself,' from the pastor's visit, I'll never understand. I kept telling him that Ben had a heart attack. I even brought the obituary of my brother, and wrote on top of the paper,

"Died of a hard-attack." I was hoping the pastor would follow up with Dad, so Dad could get things straight in his mind. However, neither the pastor nor anyone from his old church paid him a visit.

Four months following my brother's death, I was eighteen pounds heavier and two pants and dress sizes bigger. I cried out to the Lord, "Please help me to comprehend why I'm so perplexed in my overindulging with food high in sugar and gorging when I'm full?" In the quiet of my heart as I meditated and listened for guidance, I heard within me, "Stop blaming yourself; haven't you punished yourself enough?"

In the serenity of my will, God gave me insight as to why I was punishing myself. I thought I had let my niece down. I single-mindedly thought I should have encouraged Ben to give his daughter closure by admitting his wrongness in sexually abusing her. I wanted them to have the healing relationship Dad and I had found. I pondered my thoughts and became conscious that I wasn't accountable for my brother's actions, nor was it my responsibility to bring about closure in my brother's and his daughter's relationship.

"Sadness opens the heart to what was meant to be and is not. Grief opens the heart to what was not meant to be and is. Sorrow breaks the heart as it exposes the damage we've done to others as a result of our unwillingness to rely solely on the grace and truth of God."[4] Ben wasn't willing to face the man that abused him, and in not doing so Ben couldn't feel any sorrow in his heart toward his daughter. I believe before one can feel the damage they have done to others, they have to recognize the physically and emotionally damage that had happened to them.

I gave the false guilt I was carrying over to the Lord and asked for guidance on healthy eating. God revealed to me that he was the one in control and that it would be in his timetable when my niece's right of passage to her healing is disclosed. This was the beginning of an end for me; I no longer needed to be the keeper of my brother's secrets.

Six months later and thirty-five pounds lighter, I was down to size 8 petite. I can't control other people's relationships but I can control what I choose to put in my mouth. My niece's right of passage to healing is between her and God. I have no control over it but I can pray and leave the results with God.

---

[4] Page 209, *The Wounded Heart*, by Dr. Dan B. Allender.

## Chapter Fifteen

# DADDY'S BABY DAUGHTER!

"**O**ne more hurdle crossed and it looks like I'm home free," I thought as I shopped for some new summer outfits. Trying on outfit after outfit, I was excited over the big summer sales at the mall. I glanced in the mirror, liking the shapely body image that was me; I felt a feeling of accomplishment. I thanked God for getting me past the weight loss hurdle. Still, in the back of my mind I questioned, "Will the hurdles in my life ever be over?"

Summer was setting in as June filled the air with the fragrances of blossoming wild apple orchards and wild flowers along the roadside. Driving along the remote highway, I headed for town to take Dad out for lunch. I felt renewed like the warm summer day before me. Dressed in my bright, sunny yellow, short ensemble with matching anklets, I blissfully entered the building.

"Hi, Dad, ready to go?" The nurse was taking his sugar count.

"There's my baby daughter! She always liked yellow. She would call it 'yelgo'." With a chuckle he turned from talking to the nurse and tipped his brimmed brown dress hat at me. We walked down the corridor, arm and arm, with Dad singing, "Show me the way to go home..." With a big grin on his face he tipped his hat to the gals at the nursing station as out the door we went.

The following week, I received a devastating phone call concerning my dad's health. He had just suffered a massive stroke. The doctor diagnosed no recovery, with a life span left of two to six weeks at the most.

Two years prior, when Dad had had his pacemaker put in I called Lynn to inform her of his condition. Her comment was, "Funny you would even bother to call."

"You are his daughter, Lynn." She gave me some sarcastic remarks that I ignored and made my goodbyes. I kept Lynn posted over the next couple of years of Dad's health by letter. Each letter I sent out, I received one back attacking my motives and character. The animosity shown in Lynn's writings to me was only words that hadn't any effect on me other than to pray for her to heal emotionally.

Prayerfully I made a phone call to Lynn. "Hi, Lynn, it's Sam. I just called to tell you that Dad had a massive stroke. The doctor's prognosis isn't good." Click, without a word she hung up. I didn't call Lynn again. Through Dad's illness I prayerfully kept Lynn informed with postcards. Lynn and Dad's relationship was in God's hands.

Summer was just about over and Dad lingered on. School started and I was back to work. Work was good; it gave me something else to think about besides Dad's health.

Late Sunday afternoon I sat on my patio absorbed in my thoughts. I reminisced about scraping the paint off the chair with Dad. I now sat in that chair. The invigorating autumn breeze filtered through me like a cool overcast, reminding me summer is leaving. Distressed over the realism of my dad's condition, I prayed for comfort and restored confidence in my faith. Taken aback by the phone ringing in the background, I got up to answer it.

The nursing home called to tell me that my dad had a choking spell after lunch. All Dad's food was puréed so they didn't know what caused the problem. Dad quit breathing for a second or two; however, the nurse immediately did the Heimlich Maneuver on him and he instantaneously caught his breath. He didn't eat any dinner that evening. However, Dad was resting comfortably and there wasn't any emergency. The home was great in keeping us informed of Dad's health. If his sugar went up, I heard about it; if he was constipated I got a phone call; thinking about the perceptiveness of the nursing home's phone calls, I wasn't apprehensive about Dad's care.

I went to visit Dad Monday after work; I called Kenny to come to the nursing home, as Dad was worsening. Tuesday and Wednesday Dad was about the same, not eating but resting.

On Wednesday, many of the staff, mostly the young girls came in to kiss my dad goodbye and cried as they left. Dad touched many lives with his charismatic personality. He became a hugger after Jesus came into his life and he hugged everyone.

I went home late Wednesday afternoon to take a breather and replenish my energy. I bolted from the bed and caught the phone on its first ring. It was still Wednesday around 10:30 in the evening. I had slept about an hour. I recall the phone message, "come quickly." Dad was dying. I dressed and quietly slipped out of the house careful not to disturb Kenny. Praying and crying as I drove the thirty miles to the nursing home, I pleaded with God, "Please let me be with my dad when he dies, and how I long to hear him tell me one last time that he loves me."

I took Dad's hand. He never opened his eyes but gave it a little squeeze; he knew I was there. I didn't talk a whole lot but rubbed his hands, arm, and face just to let him know I was with him to sustain him through this last phase of his earthly life.

I opened Dad's Bible to where his page marker was and read Psalm 31; I tried reading to Dad, but with him so hard of hearing I didn't think he could hear me. I continued reading through the Psalms having cerebral conversations with God. I held Dad's hand with one hand and the Bible in the other. While I was communing with God, I shed many tears. Sometimes they were sobs. When Dad heard my sobs, he would move his hand a little in mine to console me. Dad started to lose some of his grip in my hand, and I knew that he was getting weaker with each breath he took; yet he kept holding on.

I set the Bible down and stood up from where I was sitting. I caressed his head and bent over to where he could hear me. In a loud whisper I said, "I love you, Daddy, I love you, Daddy", over and over I told him how much I loved him through my tears. I assured him, "I'll be all right Daddy; go in peace. Go be with Mom and Ben. They are waiting for you; I love you Daddy; I will always love you."

The nursing staff kept coming in to check on Dad; when a staff member came in, I would tell them how Dad would soon be escorted into the presence of the Lord. I would say, "Do you know that God's highest angels will come for my Dad, and the angels will escort my Dad's soul into the presence of the LORD where he will be for all eternity? Yes, Dad will soon be at God's throne not because he was a good man, but because at age sixty-eight my dad realized he was a sinner in need of a Savior. My dad asked Jesus Christ to forgive him of his sins and to come into his life and be his GOD. I know that I will see my dad again when all will be resurrected because of our faith in Christ. Jesus gave his life so that we may live." Some of the staff listened with great interest while others would listen intuitively, gradually making their exit. It seemed like hours were just fleeting by in a never-to-be-repeated timeframe.

The twilight of the night rested and a new day was thrust into our moment in time as I continued to share the gospel message. Each staff member heard the plan of salvation and how they could know for sure that they, too, could have eternal life by trusting in what Christ did on the cross in dying for all of our sins.

My dad took a deep breath. The staff member with me seemed a little alarmed. In our mind's eye he quit breathing; she made some kind of a comment that it was over when my dad took another profound breath. The staff member with me, looked up, caught my eye and swiftly vanished from the room, leaving me alone with my dad.

Approximately ten minutes after I assured my father of my well-being and love for him, he closed his eyes exceedingly tight as if a bright light was hurting his eyes. With eyes tightly closed he moved his mouth while concentrating to say something. He would do this after his stroke; he worked hard at making himself heard with endless attempts to voice his words to be understood. With eyes squeezed tightly, coming from Dad's lips he said, "I love you. I love you."

I cried, "I love you, too, Daddy." His breaths were blatant, as if each breath had a purpose, and that purpose was for my benefit. As with each peaceful breath he took, I was able to let go; subsequently he slowly slipped into eternity. "Goodbye, Daddy. I love you," I sobbed. God in his tenderness gave my dad and me our last cherished moments as a father's love for his daughter is supposed to be.

I miss my dad's constantly telling others at the nursing home, "This is my baby daughter." I miss seeing him pull out his wallet and show off my school picture. Dad's words will always be with me, "My baby daughter" and "I love you."

# Chapter Sixteen

# SHOW ME THE WAY TO GO HOME

In the morning following Dad's death, the nursing home left several messages on Lynn's answering machine telling her about her father passing on. I asked the funeral home to wait as long as they could before sending the body for cremation in case Lynn wanted to make her final farewell. Kenny and I knelt down and prayed for Lynn and her spouse prior to the funeral. Lynn never returned the calls to the nursing home nor did she attend the funeral.

At the funeral I was poised and together as I greeted old friends of Dad's and mine. However, I lost my composure when I saw Marshal, my dad's roommate and companion from the nursing home in the back of the church. Marshal's wife and son held him up; his legs were unstable and wobbly as he stumbled his way to me. Tears filled Marshal's eyes as he articulated his sympathy along with expressing the loss of his best friend.

The pastor for the service was my son-in-law, Edward, Brandy's husband. He gave an upbeat ceremony and called it a "celebration" because of Dad being with the Lord.

Randy, a colleague and friend of mine led the singing. Randy told how my dad's favorite song was, "Show me the way to go home" and how I didn't think it appealing to sing in church but he was going to sing it anyway. Everyone chucked and I cried even though I was amused.

Randy changed some of the words to the song:

> Show me the way to go home
> I'm tired and I want to go to bed
> I met the Lord and He spoke to me
> And this is what He said,
> "When your life is over
> Then Heaven you will roam"
> So wherever I go I'll be
> Singing this song
> Show me the way to go home.

Dad's old house needed cleaning out. How I dreaded that job. Kenny drove with me to the old homestead. Kenny commented on the way to Dad's house that he was going to rent a dumpster and whatever was in the garage he was throwing out as it was just old rusted tools and junk. To our amazement the garage was gutted, not a lick of useless items was in sight. We later found out that other family members of mine gutted it clean. Kenny and I had a good laugh over the incident for they must have thought they were getting something over on us when in fact it was a blessing to see it cleaned out. Jokingly I said, "Too bad I didn't leave the key in the door to the house." We had a good laugh.

I cleaned out the rubbish from inside the house. I left what I thought was usable behind. I made one last trip upstairs. Gazing out the upstairs window, the memory of my dad burying my dog flooded my mind. I flinched, went back downstairs, out the door locking it behind me, leaving behind my childhood memories of abuse.

Dad and I talked about what to do with his house and property which was put in my name back when my mother was still living. We decided to donate the property and contents to a Bible Camp nearby. I called Gary, the director of the camp. He appreciated the donation. The paperwork was drawn up and the keys were handed over.

I was on my way to the mailbox when I felt an overwhelming invasive need to pray. "Lord, please help me to be able to handle whatever comes up tonight." In the mail was a small trifling check from an insurance policy on my dad made out to me.

While walking toward the house I thought, "There isn't any amount of money that could pay for the abuse that was done to me, but then again there is no amount of money that could buy back what Dad and I had in our relationship the past several years."

Childhood memories are behind me. Only flourishing reminiscences of the journey Dad and I replaced on our way back home remain. I learned to trust my dad as he learned to deal with his abuse linked to his stepmother and in doing so Dad was able to feel the sorrow of what he had done to me.

I feel a sense of awe about me, a thankfulness beyond what I can say or put down on paper, a praise, gratefulness, a wanting to serve my God in anyway He wants me to, for I was dead and now I am alive emotionally, physically, and spiritually and all because of GOD'S wonderful compassion and grace.

## Chapter Seventeen

# LET ME GROW UP

I want to grow up!
Oh let me grow up;
It's time, you see.
It's time to spread my wings,
And be me.
Don't let me deny my feelings;
Just let me grow up.
Let me feel the pain;
Shed my cocoon.
When I arrive you'll
Like me a lot better.
If only you'll let me grow up!

I recall fearing to grow up until I got in touch with reality. Looking back, the fear was worse then the reality. My story is out. The fear, the darkness in my soul, the blackness that lined the inner me like black satin, slippery and smooth had been dealt with. At times, I seemed to have no escape or way out of the ugly haunting fear; however, the fear is out and it's over.

In recapturing many of the hurtful events of my life, I remember feeling like a wounded rabbit, soft and cuddly but timid. I tried to crawl back into my hole, more like a pit, to hide, but the deep, dark tunnel in my mind was gone and the darkness was replaced with green, grazing, grass of truth. The refreshing clover had covered my pit, and I lay out in the open with the hot sun pounding down upon my bare soft skin. My rabbit fur was covered with blood, and I felt rejected and alone because the hunter, the perpetrator, that I had trusted shot me and my wounded heart had been broken. I wasn't sure where my safety was anymore; however, I did know I didn't want to escape or hide in those dark tunnels in my mind any longer.

The sun pounded down upon me, scorching me with its heat and draining my body from all energy; however, I didn't fear death for somewhere in the heat I felt a healing power sent from the Father above.

The healer was Jesus the great physician. The healing power given through my children, husband and close friends, was agape love. Their love and acceptance of me caused me to be real and to come out of those hidden tunnels and into the open grazing grass where I was bare before them, God and myself. I started to grow and to become all that God intended me to be before the hunters, better known as perpetrators wounded the impressionable me.

On one occasion when I was at the hospital visiting my mom, when she was in intensive care, Kenny bought me a stuffed rabbit, one that was exceptionally soft and cuddly and placed the irresistible bunny in my car. Kenny said the bunny reminded him of me before I started to dredge through my past. At times, Kenny would see me get hard and cold much like my father's disposition when I was young. By putting a delusion of deadness to my emotions, I thought that I could elude the feelings that were spiraling around in my mind. When Kenny would sense the hardness in my countenance, he would take one of several bunnies I had accumulated and hand me the bunny to cuddle to soften my heart. Kenny and my conglomeration of bunnies along with the story of *Velveteen Rabbit* helped me to stay soft and pliable through the psychologically draining times.

In my struggles to grow up I questioned God's hand in my life. At times I walked away from even Him, for I often wondered where He was when all this was going on. Why didn't God protect me? Why didn't he stop the pain in my soul? However, He was there all the time bringing me gently to the point of adulthood.

# Epigraph

*Secrets of the Soul* is a modification of my journaling over many years. However, the story didn't end for the chapters of my life continue in the direction which God calls me. My goal in life is to be a witness for Jesus' love to the hurting and oppressed brought on from the consequences of abuse. Freedom comes as one faces truth and learns to be honest with himself/herself and others around him/her. Relationships are built through trust and forgiveness. I hope to be God's ambassador to point the way to truth and freedom found in knowing Jesus and his unconditional love for them. I hope to run the race and to finish the course God is directing me to go so that when I meet Jesus face to face I will hear, "Well done, faithful servant, well done." My prayer for my readers is that they will have an encounter with the Lord Jesus Christ and see themselves through His eyes. It's a promise you will like what you see and if not, than let Jesus change you from the inside.

Today, I have grown up and I happen to love the person that I have become and I have the courage to continue to develop into Christ's likeness. When I think of my dad I remember him calling me his baby daughter along with a father's actions and words of love to me in my adult life. I see the relationship that was intended for us to have; the abusive times are forgiven and behind me. I'm overwhelmed with thankfulness to God for giving me the strength to face the haunting flashbacks of childhood molestation. In my voyage to adulthood I have come to the conclusion that healing of the soul takes place when the door to the child within is opened and trust is built with a network of people who love him/her. I have given my children and grandchildren freedom from the legacy of abuse from generations past. You can do the same, if your story is one of abuse.

If you can identify with the trauma of abuse, I encourage you to seek counseling, journal, get a network of people you can trust around you or get into a support group. Support groups are listed in your local newspaper. If you are a friend or spouse of someone that has been tormented by abuse, then be a good listener. For assurance and prayer, you can email me at:

samshelleyauthor@yahoo.com

# Afterword

It has been several years since the death of my father. There has not been any contact between Lynn and me. From what I hear she has moved several hundred miles away from this area. She has found a new victim to exploit-my niece. Lynn's health isn't the greatest. I continue to pray in hope that she will make peace with her past and find the love of Jesus. I do recall times in my life when I witnessed a gentle side of Lynn. I truly believe if God could get through my tough exterior than there is still hope for my sister.

I do not anticipate having a relationship in the near future with Lynn or Louie. One can forgive someone for the wrong done to them, but that does not mean they can trust that person and move back into the relationship. Forgiving someone doesn't make what he/she did right, but it gives you freedom from the pain that was caused by him/her. Circumstances are out of my control, but I can choose happiness beyond the circumstances.

# Bibliography

## Building Self Image

Christenson, Larry. *The Renewed Mind*. Minneapolis: Bethany House Publishers, 1981.

Matzat, Don. *Christ Esteem*. Oregon: Harvest House Publishers, 1990.

McDowell, Josh. *His Image My Image*. CA: Here's Life Publishers Inc., 1984.

Wagner, Th.M.,Ph. D. Maurice E. *The Sensation of Being Somebody*. Grand Rapids: Zondervan Publishing House, 1975.

## Emotions

Backus, William, and Marie Chapian. *Telling Yourself The Truth*. Minneapolis: Bethany House Publishers, 1980.

Carter, Les. *Good 'N' Angry*. Grand Rapids: Baker Book House, 1983.

Carter, Les. *Mind Over Emotions*. Grand Rapids: Baker Book House, 1985.

Dobson, Dr. James. *Emotions, Can You Trust Them.* CA: Regal Books, 1980.

Lutzer, Erwin. *Managing Your Emotions.* Weaton: Victor Books, 1985.

Minirth, M.D. Frank B. and Paul D. Meier, M.D. *Happiness Is A Choice.* Grand Rapids: Baker Book House, 1978.

Potter-Efron, Ronald, and Patricia Potter-Efron. *Letting Go Of Shame.* MN: Hazelden, 1989.

Schmidt, Jerry A. *Do You Hear What You're Thinking.* Weaton: Victor Books, 1973.

Seamands, David A. *Healing for Damaged Emotions.* Weaton: Victor Books, 1983.

Seamands, David A. *Healing of Memories.* Weaton: Victor Books, 1978

Thurman, Chris. *The Lies We Believe.* Nashville: Thomas Nelson Publishers, 1982.

## Relationships

Carter, Dr. Les. *Imperative People.* Nashville: Thomas Nelson Publishers, 1991.

Chapman, Gary. *The Five Love Languages.* Chicago: Northfield Publishing, 1995.

Cloud, Dr. Henry, and Dr. John Townsend. *Boundaries.* Grand Rapids: Zondervan Publishing House, 1992.

Ellis, Alfred. *One-Way Relationships.* Nashville: Thomas Nelson Publishers, 1990.

Hemfelt, Dr. Robert, Dr. Frank Minirth, and Dr. Paul Meier. *Love Is A Choice.* Nashville: Thomas Nelson Publishers, 1989.

Hemfelt, Dr. Robert, and Dr. Paul Warren. *Kids Who Carry Our Pain.* Nashville: Thomas Nelson Publishers, 1990.

## Sexual Abuse

Allender, Dr. Dan B. *The Wounded Heart.* Colorado Springs: NavPress, 1990.

Caruso, Beverly. *The Impact of Incest.* MN: Hazelden, 1987.

Frank, Jan. *A Door of Hope.* CA: Here's Life Publishers, 1987.

Hancock, Maxine, and Karen Burton Mains. *Child Sexual Abuse: A Hope for Healing.* Wheaton: Harold Shaw Publishers, 1987.

Peters, David B. *A Betrayal Of Innocence: What Everyone Should Know About Child Sexual Abuse.* TX: Word Books, Inc., 1986.

Lew, Mike. *Victims No Longer.* New York: Nevraumont Publishing Co.,1986.

Maltz, Wendy, and Beverly Holman. *Incest and Sexuality: A Guide to Understanding and Healing.* MA: Lexington Books, 1987.

# The Author

S am Shelley is a Bible teacher, speaker and workshop leader. Shelley lives in Michigan with her husband. She has four children, two biological and two adopted. She now has nine grandchildren. Sam is currently working with the emotionally impaired in a classroom setting.

Printed in the United States
28777LVS00001B/421-672

9 781597 811781